GW01339516

Hunting the Clean Boot

BRIAN LOWE

Hunting the Clean Boot

THE WORKING BLOODHOUND

FOREWORD BY PHIL DRABBLE

BLANDFORD PRESS
Poole   Dorset

First published in the U.K. 1981 by
Blandford Press,
Link House, West Street,
Poole, Dorset, BH15 1LL

Copyright © 1981 Blandford Books Ltd

British Library Cataloguing in Publication Data

Lowe, Brian
   Hunting the clean boot. – (Adventure sports series).
   1. Bloodhounds
   I. Title II. Series
   636.7'53   SF429.B6

ISBN 0 7137 0950 2

All rights reserved. No part of this book may be reproduced or transmitted in any form or by any means, electronic or mechanical, including photocopying, recording or any information storage and retrieval system, without permission in writing from the Publisher.

Set in 11/13pt Baskerville and printed and bound in Great Britain by Fakenham Press Limited, Fakenham, Norfolk

Contents

Acknowledgements		vii
Foreword		ix
Preface		xi
1	History of the Bloodhound	1
2	Acquiring and Training a Puppy	34
3	The Standard – Function, Fault or Fancy	74
4	Working Trials	105
5	Comments from Experienced Huntsmen	154
6	Bloodhounds for Police and Army Work	179
Appendix 1: Kennel Club Working Trial Rules for Bloodhounds		225
Appendix 2: Some Useful Addresses		228
Glossary		229
Index		232

Acknowledgements

My grateful thanks go to the following for their contributions and help in the preparation of this book:
Bobbie Edwards, Hon. Secretary of the Bloodhound Club, Hon. Secretary of the Hound Association, Bloodhound Breed Representative to the Breed and Working Trial Kennel Club Liaison Councils, for her work with camera and tape recorder and for her contributions of Chapter 2 and a large part of Chapter 4. It is her valuable knowledge and assistance which has helped to make this book possible. Eric Furness M.H.; Lady Rosemary Brudenell Bruce; Leonarda Pogodzinski, Hon. Working Trials Secretary of the Association of Bloodhound Breeders; Ex-Sergeant Major George Yeandle B.E.M.; Reg R. Wright M.H.; David L. Kingsberry M.R.C.V.S.; Major W. Stringer M.H., Chairman of the Master of Bloodhounds Association; The Kennel Club of Great Britain; The American Kennel Club; Lieutenant-Colonel Keith Morgan Jones; Chief Inspector Wilkinson; Laurie Denny; Colonel and Mrs A. J. C. Seymour; Mr and Mrs Joe Chamberlain; Jane Crease; Margaret Lowe for her patience and help with the manuscript; American Bloodhound Club for permission to reproduce the article from the *American Bloodhound Bulletin*; Phyllis Natanek; Susan R. Bennett; Robin O'Neil; Mr and Mrs R. M. Brooks; Sir Rupert Buchanan-Jardine Bt.

The author and publisher would also like to thank the following for their kind permission to reproduce photographs and illustrations:

British Library, 5, 6; Trustees of the British Museum, 3; Ron Burton/Daily Mirror, Endpapers; Butt Studio, Bourton-on-the-Water, 30; Coventry Evening Telegraph, 155; Anne Cumbers, 26; Colin Jones, 28; The Kennel Club, xii, 18–20, 35, 109, 193, 195, 198; Patrick McGuiness, 181; E. C. Ockenden/Bracknell and Wokingham Times Group, 11; Ordnance Survey map and photographs reproduced with the permission of the Controller of H.M.S.O. Crown copyright reserved, 148–151; Anne Roslin-Williams, 32; The Sherlock Holmes Public House, 191; Sport and General Press Agency, 160, 175; Yorkshire Evening Press, 53.

The drawings on pp. 88–103 are by Anita Lawrence, based on the originals by Phyllis Natanek.

Foreword

Bloodhounds are among the most affectionate and gentle breeds of dog. Brian Lowe is at pains to point out the fact in *Hunting the Clean Boot* and I have often confirmed it from my own experience.

But don't be fooled by that! Hunting with hounds stirs deep rooted, primitive instincts and a pack of bloodhounds, in full cry, will excite the most unimaginative.

This was driven home to me the first time I was asked to be the runner to lay a line for Reg Wright's hounds to hunt on television. Instead of laying the line some time before it was hunted, the producer decided it would be more dramatic if hounds caught up with me in full view of cameras.

I knew the hounds individually. They were delightfully friendly. Reg assured me that they would be equally pleased to see me, in hot blood, at the end of the chase.

But I freely admit that, when I heard that pack of hounds chime out like a peal of bells and realised that I was their quarry, the hair stood up on the nape of my neck!

That is half the fun with bloodhounds. They provide all the thrills of the chase without the blood and gore.

Brian Lowe is steeped in bloodhound lore and thoroughly in tune with bloodhound men, some of whom have contributed to his book.

His enthusiasm is so contagious that strangers to his art cannot fail to become infected and tempted to keep bloodhounds for themselves.

So the book does not minimise the snags. 'Bloodhounds slobber and die of bloat. They jump up friends and muddy their clothes. They are difficult to train and have bad eyes.' The faint hearted will be put off before they begin, as Brian Lowe intends. Nothing could be worse than that his beloved hounds should get a bad name because they were kept by a bad owner.

But, for the genuine enthusiasts, who fall in love with them, warts and all, this is the book. It traces the history and folklore of hunting dogs back to our primitive ancestors, who hunted more for food than for sport. It uncovers the mysteries of unravelling trails so cold and difficult that lesser breeds would be lost before they had begun, and advises on handling hounds from puppyhood to competitive trials.

Having sampled the delights of hunting the clean boot across wild and beautiful countryside myself, I have no hesitation in advising others to do the same. But I will lay odds that, if they are persuaded to act as runners and lay the trail, the sound of hounds on their line will send shivers down their spines!

Phil Drabble
October 1980

Preface

This book will, I hope, help to foster an interest in the bloodhound as a working breed and, at the same time, introduce new people to an unusual and most enjoyable sport. Hunting the clean boot is a true country activity, offering the full excitement of the hunt whether carried out on a modest scale with one hound or on a grand scale with a whole pack, and it is a sport that can be enjoyed by anyone with a love of hounds and the countryside.

After many a discussion on hunting bloodhounds, following an exhausting windswept day at a trials and over a meal with a warming bottle of wine, I finally decided to pull together some of the many opinions and anecdotes I had heard from experienced masters, huntsmen and bloodhound handlers over the years. This book is the result of that endeavour and will, I hope, offer both a practical guide to those readers who might wish to try their hand, and an accumulation of entertaining information for those with a more passive interest in the sport.

Comment has been made on the present show scene, but only in a limited form since I believe that the best way to judge hounds is to follow them and observe them in action over some distance, giving them a chance to show the fitness and soundness of movement which no self-respecting hound, given the choice, would be without.

I dedicate this work to all bloodhounds that hunt and thank them for the many years of pleasure they have given me in this sport in the English countryside. In particular, I remember my own hounds, one of whom, Shylock of Stanwell, I still hear and see vividly whenever I am near open country or park land.

Brian Lowe
Surbiton
Surrey
November 1979

Edwin Brough and hound.

1
History of the Bloodhound

> 'O'er all, the bloodhound boasts superior skill,
> To scent, to view, to turn, and boldly kill–
> His fellows' vain alarms rejects with scorn,
> True to the master's voice and learned horn;–
> His nostrils oft, if ancient fame sings true,
> Traced the sly felon thro' the tainted dew;
> Once snuff'd, he follows with unaltered aim,
> Nor odours lure him from the chosen game;
> Deep-mouth'd, he thunders, and inflamed he views,
> Springs on relentless, and to death pursues.'
>
> *Thomas Tickell* (1686–1740)

If the subject of the bloodhound is to be taken at all seriously it is important to know and understand the historical background behind this romantic and much misunderstood animal.

There are a number of reference books that have been written on this subject, all of them worthy of consideration, but one small pocket companion *The Bloodhound and Its Use in Tracking Criminals* by Edwin Brough, first published in 1902 for the now extinct *Illustrated Kennel News*, is in my view, the best informed work. Unfortunately, it is now out of print.

Brough's major contribution to the study of the breed was his research into the work of the Count Le Couteulx de Canteleu, a great nineteenth-century authority on bloodhounds. This study helped to form the basis on which Brough formulated the Bloodhound Standard which is used to this day.

Before referring to some extracts from Brough's book, I think it useful to cover the earlier history of the bloodhound which is important if we are to see its full perspective. I would not like to stick my neck out too far when asserting my own opinion as to the origin of the bloodhound, but there are a number of ideas as to where the oldest recorded time and place may be.

Early Origins

It is generally believed that the ancestral home of the bloodhound was Assyria in Mesopotamia. The kings of Assyria around 2000–1000 B.C. bred dogs for hunting and warfare which are frequently found depicted on terracotta or stone reliefs of that period. The resemblance of these ancient hounds to the present-day bloodhound is evident.

It is probable that the Assyrian dogs were taken to the shores of the Mediterranean by the sea-faring Phoenicians and from there, spread northwards through present-day Europe. Two notable concentrations of hounds developed in Gaul in the seventh and eighth centuries A.D. One was in Brittany, and the other, more important, was in the Ardennes area of Northern France. It was from this latter group that the famous St Huberts, thought to be the direct ancestor of the bloodhound, arose.

Much of this early history is pure conjecture based on the little evidence available, and there are many different views on the subject. Indeed, some authorities believe that the bloodhound ancestor was to be found in Britain before the sixth century A.D. However, although the very earliest history is lost to us, I think it is likely that the St Hubert hound was involved at some time and I shall therefore start with the story of St Hubert and his hounds.

St Hubert

The story of St Hubert, after whom the hounds of the Ardennes were named, is fascinating, and anyone with an interest in bloodhounds will certainly wish to know it. François Hubert, the son of a wealthy Ardennes nobleman of the seventh century, had a

An Assyrian hunting dog carved in relief on a stone slab, c. 650 B.C., from the palace of Ashurbanipal at Nineveh.

passion for the chase and bred a number of excellent hounds for his sport. He lived happily with his wife Floribane in great luxury. However, this happiness was not to last and was suddenly ended by the early death of Floribane. After this, Hubert found little pleasure in life and devoted practically all his time to hunting.

One Good Friday, when hunting in the woods near his home, he was suddenly confronted by the miraculous appearance of a stag bearing a glittering crucifix between its antlers. This vision was to completely change Hubert's life, and after much contemplation he gave up all his riches and entered a monastery. This conversion has been used on many occasions as a subject for paintings by famous artists.

After several years of monastic life, Hubert went on a long

pilgrimage to Rome, as a result of which he was appointed Bishop of Tongern. He was later made Bishop of Liege where he built a beautiful cathedral. In A.D. 825, nearly one hundred years after his death, Hubert was canonised as the patron saint of hunters, and his body, which had miraculously remained intact, was removed with due ceremony to a Benedictine cloister in his native Ardennes.

It is interesting to note that in France there is an ancient custom associated with St Hubert's Day (3 November), in which the priest blesses the pack collectively after Mass. He then blesses separately the oldest member of the hunt, the oldest horse and the oldest hound, attaching a red rosette to the buttonhole of the man, and to the neck of the horse and of the hound. St Hubert's Day is still celebrated in France, Belgium and Ireland and still includes a blessing of the hounds.

The St Hubert Hound

After the death of St Hubert successive abbots and monks preserved his strain of hounds, which were at first black, later developing small tan markings and eventually becoming black and tan.

The Count Le Couteulx de Canteleu described these hounds thus:

> They were deep-throated, fine-nosed hounds showing great powers of endurance, but not necessarily great swiftness, and were very courageous and daring. They were chiefly prized as limiers for unharbouring the wild boar and were generally of a slightly reddish-black, with tan marks over the eyes and on the legs and feet, with long pendulous ears, well shaped, but rather long loins not so high on the leg as the Normandy hound.

The black and tan St Huberts were used as limiers for wolf and boar, and were noted for their courage, endurance and voice. From 1220 to 1798 the abbots of St Hubert presented three couples of these hounds yearly to the Kings of France as a token of allegiance.

As well as the black and tan St Huberts there were some white hounds, which, although larger, were never as popular because they would only hunt the stag.

In the twelfth and thirteenth centuries there were additions to the St Hubert strains from crusaders travelling back from the Holy Land.

The hounds were introduced into England by William the Conqueror in 1066, and in later years some of these with the additional strains developed a solid greyish-red colour, becoming known as 'Dunne Houndes'. In the sixteenth century, chocolate-coloured hounds made their first appearance and it was not until the nineteenth century that the true St Hubert strain died out.

It is thought that the white St Huberts were probably crossed with other white French hounds to produce the famous early

St Hubert hound (from *The Noble Art of Venerie* or *Hunting*, London 1576).

Talbot hounds. These were introduced into England with the black and tan St Huberts by William the Conqueror and the Talbot family who came from Normandy. The coat of arms of this family, who were later the Earls of Shrewsbury, has two white Talbot hounds supporting the escutcheon. There are many inn signs portraying these hounds to be found in England, especially in Somerset and Gloucestershire. The Talbot hound flourished in the Middle Ages but died out in Europe in the sixteenth century and in England in the nineteenth century.

The Talbot hound has been described as follows:

> This hound has a round thick head, with a short nose uprising. Large open nostrils. Ears exceedingly large and thin, and down hanging much lower than his chaps. The flews of his upper lips are

Talbot hound (from *The Noble Art of Venerie* or *Hunting*, London 1576).

almost two inches lower than his nether chaps; back long and straight. Huckle bones round and hidden. Thighs round. Hams straight. Tail long and rush grown – that is, big at the setting on, and small downwards. Legs large and lean, foot high-knuckled, and well clawed, with dry hard sole. Such was the ancient hound, the ancestor of our modern Bloodhound.

Use of Sleuth-hounds

In mediaeval times sleuth, slot or slough hounds (from Slot, meaning to track), were much used by nightwatchman on curfew patrol against the ever-present terror of footpads. From the twelfth century onwards bishops rode to hounds, as did many of the Church dignitaries. During this time most monasteries kept their own packs, and the breeding of hounds was carried out carefully and selectively.

However, it was in the sixteenth and seventeenth centuries that hounds were really first used to hunt man, particularly on the Scottish borders against sheep stealers and poachers. Hounds could by right of law follow trails anywhere, including even into houses with complete impunity.

In border warfare the sleuth-hound played a most important part. When the beacon-fire blazed, the country rose; all men, on horse or foot, were bound, upon pain of death, to follow the fray with 'Hue and Cry' (Hue, a loud outcry, from the French word *Huer*, to hoot): the 'Slogan' was sounded, and the pursuit by 'Hot Trodd' (from Hot, meaning recent or fresh and Trodd, meaning to step or walk on) rapidly made. The laws of Queen Elizabeth I in 1563 still permitted the custom of the Marches of pursuit by the aggrieved parties by 'Lawful Trodd with Hound and Horn, with Hue and Cry, and all other accustomed manner of fresh pursuit, for the recovery of their goods spoiled'. The offender could be lawfully pursued in Hot Trodd by the warden of either kingdom into the opposite realm, and, if overtaken and apprehended, brought back. The pursuit was often followed with a lighted turf carried on a spear.

The sleuth-hound of that time was so heavy and slow that he was often taken up and carried on the saddle bow for a time when the pursuers came to soft ground where the trail was visible. If the horse of that period was faster than the hound, the latter must have indeed been slow.

According to Edwin Brough, it was during the sixteenth century that the name of bloodhound first came into use, although some authorities claim that it was used much earlier in Norman times. Brough believed that when, in the mid-1500s, fox hunting was introduced as a replacement for stag hunting, which had declined following the gradual destruction of the great deer parks, the old sleuth-hound was found to be too slow for this new sport. To replace it, a new, faster hound was bred by crossing the Talbot with the greyhound, producing a hound specifically developed for fox hunting. In order to distinguish between the two types of hound, it became usual to refer to the old sleuth-hound as the bloodhound, meaning the hound of pure blood, as opposed to the new foxhound, which was bred from various strains. Contrary to popular belief, the name bloodhound, therefore, has nothing to do with ferocity or the ability to follow a trail of blood.

Other well-known names for bloodhounds were limier, lyme-ho or lymer, because they were led on a line or leach or lyam when nearing their quarry. Brache was a gentlemanly term used for the Talbot bitches, the dogs being referred to as Racks.

Bloodhound Packs

During the first half of the nineteenth century the bloodhound seems to have fallen out of use in England both for man-hunting and for the hunting of animals. At that time they were mostly kept in packs.

In the 1870s Lord Wolverton hunted turned out red deer in the county of Dorset with a pack of bloodhounds, and Whyte-Melville, in his *Riding Recollections*, describes them as:

> Full, sonorous, and musical, it is not extravagant to compare these deep mouthed notes with the peal of an organ in a cathedral. Yet

they run a tremendous pace. Stride, courage, and condition (the last essential requiring constant care), enable them to sustain such speed over the open as to make a good horse look foolish; while amongst enclosures they charge the fences in line like a squadron of heavy dragoons. Yet, for all this fire and mettle in chase, they are sad cowards under pressure from a crowd. A whip cracked hurriedly, a horse, galloping in their track even at an injudicious rate, will make the best of them shy and sulky for half the day.

When Lord Wolverton gave up his pack in 1879, Lord Carrington hunted them in Buckinghamshire for one season before the greater part of the pack was taken over by the Count Le Couteulx de Canteleu. The Count had previously hunted with hounds for many years and his kennel list for 1876/7 tells of 'Names remembered, because they, living, can ne'er be dead'. The list contains names such as Holford's Regent and Matchless, Becker's Brenda and Duchess, Cowen's Druid and Dewlap, Pease's Druid, Jenning's Tiger, Fury and Druid; the last was sold to Prince Napoleon. The best of hounds around 1900 were full of this blood.

The Count never tired of singing their praises: 'I have never seen more beautiful hounds nor keener ones. The way they killed deer and wild boar was admirable, but unfortunately the boars killed too many for me'.

It is interesting to note that a St Hubert hound appears in one of the pedigrees in the above kennel list. This must have been one of the last of the breed, as it became extinct about that time.

Not everyone of that period agreed that bloodhounds made good pack hounds. Mr J. Nevill Fitt (one of our must reliable authorities) expressed the following views on the subject:

> I do not consider these good hounds for a pack because each hunts for himself, and they do not look to and depend on each other. Moreover to form an efficient pack hounds must at times be taken hold of by the huntsman, and turned by the whip. This bloodhounds do not like. I heard Lord Wolverton say the same, and my own experience bears it out. They are too independent or clever, if the term is more agreeable to their admirers; and I fear that I must add that this – cleverness is at times so great as to border very closely on contrariness. It is not so much inferiority of

nose, as want of patience and method in using it that debars most dogs, more particularly hounds from hunting as cold a scent as a bloodhound. Let him work and drive like the foxhound, and he would no longer hunt a man or deer hours after he had been gone.

My opinion of a bloodhound is that he is out of place in a pack; but that, used as the Hon. Crantley Berkeley used Druid, either to drive game to the rifle or to retrieve it when wounded, they are invaluable. Here using one or a couple as the case may be, their cleverness and independence has full scope; they can use their intellect without interference from a huntsman, take time to puzzle out a scent when at fault, and hunt after their own manner; but this is not what we want in a pack.

Edwin Brough agreed with Mr Nevill Fitt when it came to the use of bloodhounds for driving game:

> In the Galtee mountains, Co. Tipperary, the bloodhound is found to be of great service in driving fallow deer to the guns. These mountains are very thickly wooded, and deer-stalking as in Scotland, is quite impracticable. Eight or ten beaters are used and the rifles are posted at likely crossing places, and the woods beaten backwards and forwards, the deer generally breaking back. The keeper who has charge of the bloodhounds walks on a ride in line with the beat, leading the hound. Directly a good buck is seen the hound is put on the line, still on the lead. The keeper carries a signal horn, with which to intimate to the guns the finding of a likely deer, and then the interesting houndwork begins, though it is no sinecure for the keeper. With this method the guns are certain of a shot before long. The hound does not give tongue, except on viewing deer.

Fine Nose and Freedom from Change

The old writers all seem agreed that the speciality of bloodhounds is that they have a more delicate nose and can hunt a lighter scent than any other hound, and that they are especially 'free from change', i.e. they will never change from the hunted animal to a fresh one.

Major W. A. Stringer M.H. and the Windsor Forest Bloodhound Pack (and hunt terrier 'Shorty'!), one of the some half dozen remaining bloodhound packs in Britain today.

In *Horse and the Hound* by Nimrod (Chas. Apperley), published in 1842, we read that the bloodhound:

> possessed the property of unerringly tracing the scent he was laid upon, amongst a hundred others; which evinces a superiority, at all events a peculiarity, of nose entirely unknown to our lighter hounds of any breed. The want of being able to distinguish the hunted fox from a fresh found one is the bane of English fox-hunting, and there are not wanting those who think that, in the breeding of the modern foxhound, the minor points of high form and blood are more frequently considered than they should be in preference of a regard to nose.

Mr J. Nevill Fitt says:

> Whether the bloodhound can really hunt a lower scent than ordinary hounds will, I fancy, always be a moot point; there is no doubt but he has an exceedingly fine nose, and nature has endowed him with the patience to make the most of it. My own idea is that a bloodhound simply hunts a colder scent than a foxhound because he takes more pains. He stoops for a scent when the other is driven ahead. It is like the quick schoolboy and the plodding one; they are each very well in their place – that of the foxhound being to chase his victim to death as quickly as possible, the bloodhound to hunt it down by patience and perseverance.

Ferocious Slave Hunters?

It is a popular myth that the hounds used to track down runaway slaves in the Southern States of America during the last century were bloodhounds. In fact, these hounds were trained to pull down their man and it is not possible to do this with a bloodhound.

Brough comments:

> His majestic appearance and docile disposition gained him many friends, though amongst the uninformed he was and is sometimes regarded as a ferocious monster endowed with miraculous scenting attributes; capable of pursuing his victim successfully under any conditions till caught, when he would certainly tear him limb from limb. This may probably be accounted for partly by his name, which is calculated to inspire awe and partly by recollections of slave hunting tales in Uncle Tom's Cabin. As a matter of fact, the hounds used for slave hunting in the Southern States of America, although called bloodhounds, were not bloodhounds at all, but merely the foxhound of the country, sometimes crossed with the Cuban mastiff, or, as it was sometimes called, the Cuban bloodhound.
>
> This last animal had no right to be called a bloodhound, or in fact a hound at all, and was more like an inferior Great Dane than anything else, though it is not believed that it ever attained to any really fixed type.

Infusion of New Blood

Towards the end of the nineteenth century there were several outcrosses made in an attempt to strengthen the breed. However, the most successful infusion of new blood was that introduced by Mr E. Nichols in 1876. This originated from the New Forest in the South of England where hounds had been kept since the days of William Rufus. Until 1898 each keeper in the New Forest was allowed to keep a couple of hounds on his walk (area of charge) and although these were called Talbots, they were evidently degenerate bloodhounds. One keeper, named Maynard, on the Beaulieu walk used to boast that the breed had been handed down in his family from father to sons for more than 300 years.

Around 1840–50, Mr Thomas Nevill of Chilland, near Winchester, procured one or two couples of New Forest hounds from Primer, the keeper on the Boldrewood walk, and from them originated a small pack which he used for hunting. Mr Nevill is reputed to have hunted practically everything and anything including deer, fox, hare and even water rat in the off-season. He also hunted a tame jackal which was chased for many a mile, and then returned to the hearthrug when the hunt was over. Mr Nevill wanted to get his hounds as black as possible – marked like black and tan terriers – and this he achieved in his lifetime.

About the time of Mr Nevill's death, Mr Nichols bought a bitch named Countess from this kennel, and from her bred a bitch called Restless by Mr E. Reynold's Ray's Victor. Restless was sent to a great dog called Luath XI, and produced the grandest litter of bloodhounds bred up to that time. Mr Nichols reared ten or eleven of the puppies to about twelve months old, and then sold most of them for large prices. Unfortunately, some of the best of these died without having been exhibited, but among those remaining were Bravo, Lawyer, Ch. Napier, and the three bitches of the litter – Belladonna, Hebe and Diana, all champions. The success of this outcross was so evident that it was impossible at the turn of the century to find a pure-bred bloodhound without much of this blood in his veins.

Brough comments on this development:

Of late years [the end of the last century and the beginning of this], the bloodhound has been bred on more galloping lines, and is a very much faster hound than he was in moss-trooping [seventeenth-century border poaching] days, his feet are rounder and more knuckled up. His characteristic head formation has been well maintained, and the general average of excellence greater than it was fifty years ago [1850s].

Today's Bloodhound

After World War 2, the breed became scarce again; in fact there were only six registrations made with the Kennel Club in 1944. However, another important outcross was arranged in the early 1950s which helped to rebuild the breed. This outcross involved a Dumfriesshire foxhound, Dumfriesshire Spendthrift, mated to a bloodhound dog, Ch. Coral of Westsummerland.

However, Spendthrift was by no means a pure-bred foxhound. The Dumfriesshire foxhounds were a pack of orthodox foxhounds when they were taken over by Sir John Buchanan-Jardine in 1924, but he decided that he wanted a pack of black and tan hounds with low scenting qualities and a very deep voice. This was accomplished by crossing the foxhounds with bloodhounds and French hounds. Dumfriesshire Spendthrift was by a pure bloodhound (Castle Milk Horsa) out of a black and tan Dumfriesshire bitch (Solace).

The Spendthrift × Coral outcross was very successful and produced, within a very few generations, two of the finest bloodhounds ever bred. These were Ch. The Cheyenne of Brighton and Ch. Delburn Buccaneer who were descended through the Peak Bloodhounds back to Dumfriesshire Spendthrift, and who won more Challenge Certificates at shows than any other hounds. This is a good example of the quality to be gained through the careful use of outcrossing.

The other method of revitalising the breed is to import hounds from other countries. For example, Westsummerland Montgomery of Bre-Mar-Har-Ros was imported from Canada to

A Dumfriesshire Foxhound – Sailor. Note the difference between the shape of the head of this hound and that of a bloodhound. This particular hound is lighter in colour than most Dumfriesshire Foxhounds, they are usually dark black and tan like the Doberman, being tan only on cheeks, legs and chest with virtually no white.

Britain and gave some good virile stock, producing several champions. Other notable imports were Barsheen Bynda of Hugenot, The Chase's Mimsy of Brighton, Knightcall's Black Cherry and Abingerwood Lime Tree Pendragon all from the USA, and Barsheen Ozannah de la Meutre d'Autrefois from Belgium.

However, I believe that care should be taken not to over-use these imports in lieu of outcrossing. The tendency will be to prefer imports for economic reasons, since although it is expensive to purchase and transport stock, it is far more expensive to outcross.

This is because, following an outcross, a breeder must raise five generations of pups in order to produce a hound eligible for registration with the Kennel Club. The amount of time, money and skill required to do this, is colossal.

Many people believe that an outcross is currently necessary and I think that it would certainly do no harm to the bloodhound and if successful, would be of great benefit to the breed. After all, Brough thought that an outcross was desirable every fifth generation to retain vigour and soundness in the breed.

Shows and Trials

The introduction of dog shows in England in 1859 and their great popularity certainly helped to save the bloodhound breed from extinction. Shows rapidly became fashionable in Victorian society and dog breeding gained commercial interest.

The first public bloodhound working trials were held at Warwick in 1886 but were very elementary. Three years later, trials were again attempted at the Kennel Club Show in London and at Dublin Dog Show but these did not prove successful and the idea was dropped until the formation of the Association of Bloodhound Breeders in 1897.

The following comment on breeding bloodhounds for shows or trials was made by Brough at the turn of the century:

> The greatest benefactor to the ancient race is the man who breeds intelligently, and supports both trials and shows, but there will always be people who are unable to devote time to both, and the trialer should remember that he will always be greatly indebted to the showman, and the showman should bear in mind that he owes the excuse for his existance to the trialer. Both are equally interested in maintaining the true type, and their conception of the ideal hound should be the same.
>
> Of late years it has become a fashion in some quarters to profess to believe that dogs of any kind, which are successful on the bench, must necessarily be useless for work, and this belief is sometimes most strongly held by those who have not specially distinguished

Possible Derivation of the Present-day Bloodhound

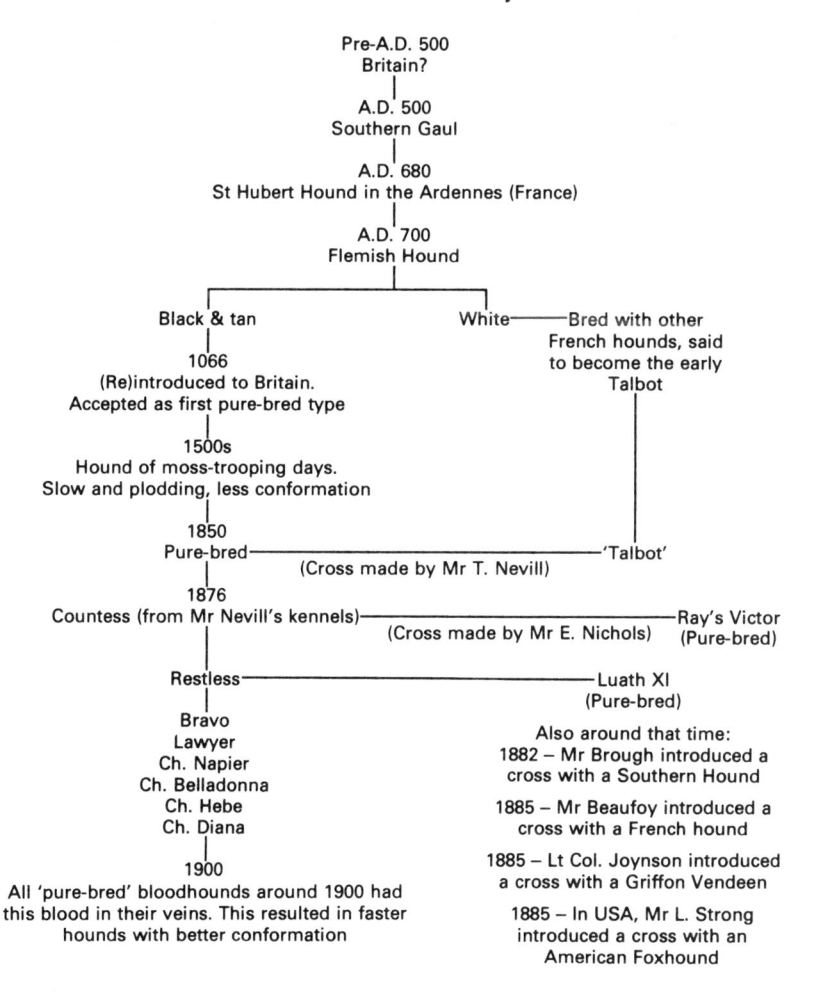

Pre-A.D. 500
Britain?
|
A.D. 500
Southern Gaul
|
A.D. 680
St Hubert Hound in the Ardennes (France)
|
A.D. 700
Flemish Hound
|
┌─────────────────────────────┴─────────────────────────────┐
Black & tan   White────────Bred with other
| French hounds, said
1066   to become the early
(Re)introduced to Britain.   Talbot
Accepted as first pure-bred type
|
1500s
Hound of moss-trooping days.
Slow and plodding, less conformation
|
1850
Pure-bred ── 'Talbot'
| (Cross made by Mr T. Nevill)
1876
Countess (from Mr Nevill's kennels)─────────────────────────Ray's Victor
| (Cross made by Mr E. Nichols)   (Pure-bred)
Restless ──────────────────────────── Luath XI
| (Pure-bred)
Bravo
Lawyer   Also around that time:
Ch. Napier   1882 – Mr Brough introduced a
Ch. Belladonna   cross with a Southern Hound
Ch. Hebe
Ch. Diana   1885 – Mr Beaufoy introduced a
| cross with a French hound
1900
All 'pure-bred' bloodhounds around 1900 had   1885 – Lt Col. Joynson introduced
this blood in their veins. This resulted in faster   a cross with a Griffon Vendeen
hounds with better conformation
                                               1885 – In USA, Mr L. Strong
                                               introduced a cross with an
                                               American Foxhound

After World War 2

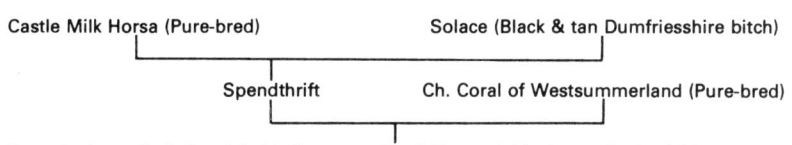

Castle Milk Horsa (Pure-bred)   Solace (Black & tan Dumfriesshire bitch)
└──────────────────────┬──────────────────────────────────┘
         Spendthrift   Ch. Coral of Westsummerland (Pure-bred)
         └────────────────────────┬──────────────────────┘
                                  |
Hounds almost indistinguishable from pure-bred. Two notable descendants of this outcross were Ch. The Cheyenne of Brighton and Ch. Delburn Buccaneer; two of the finest bloodhounds ever bred.

The first bloodhound trials held by the Association of Bloodhound Breeders (A.B.B.) in the late 1890s were organised in great secrecy; none of the competitors knowing the venue beforehand. The event was enjoyed by a large crowd of spectators.

themselves in breeding exhibition animals. Fortunately, the bloodhound has not fallen a victim to the freaks of the 'fancier', and although his remarkable head characteristics have been somewhat accentuated of late years they have not been altered in any way. Doubtless there are good workers which have not sufficient type and quality for the bench, but many of the most successful show hounds have proved themselves the best workers also when they have had opportunities of showing their capability, and this is only what is natural to expect.

The only innovations are that the bloodhound is now a much faster hound than formerly, and that his feet are rounder and more knuckled up. Originally the bloodhound had a long hare foot. It is to be hoped that these changes are wholly advantageous, and there do not seem to be any indications to the contrary, but it is always dangerous to tamper with the characteristics of a breed. An

The first A.B.B. trials proved a great success, arousing considerable interest around Britain and receiving extensive press coverage, such as this illustration entitled 'Bloodhounds on the trail. The man-hunting experiments in Yorkshire'.

Early twentieth-century bloodhound trials on Salisbury Plain. Photograph 6 shows two hounds starting a line in the Couple Stake.

increased pace may at first seem a useful benefit but it should be remembered that it is only so if it does not dilute from the special nose and mental ability of the bloodhound.

Edwin Brough is considered by many well informed enthusiasts in Britain today to be a source of much of the authoritative information on bloodhounds. However, we must bear in mind that, as authoritative as Brough's knowledge and comment was, it was pertinent to the date written. It would appear from my own observations that if Brough were to see some hounds of the present day he might well have fitting comment to make!

Brough's article was first published in the *Illustrated Kennel News* in 1902, still in the days of horse-drawn transport. Since then, we have had two World Wars, an advance in technology never dreamt of at that time, bringing with it marketing, the mass media and commercialism on a grand scale which has inevitably had an influence on animal breeding throughout the world. Dog shows have mushroomed and the market for pet food products is worth a considerable amount of money.

It is very easy to look in at almost any show and see the exaggeration in breeding that has produced accentuated types for cosmetic purposes. It is fair to say that as a result of this interference some breeds would not be able to survive long in procreative terms left to their own devices as they would not pass Mother Nature's stringent test in the laws of survival.

Fortunately, the bloodhound has not fallen victim to the pressure of this century in quite the same sad way as some breeds. However, he has nevertheless erred from the original Standard set by Brough and his colleague Dr Sidney Turner and there is a tendency, generally speaking, to prefer exaggeration of type. He suffers from a number of disorders peculiar to large breeds and in particular his own special malady, that of bad eyes, for which there is no excuse. Showing should be essentially in the interest of sound healthy breeding as well as fostering the enthusiasm of the owner.

Working Trial Champions since World War 2

WT Ch. Raycroft Jailer

Easebourne Senator
    Am. & Eng. Ch. Spotter of Littlebrook
        Operator of White Isle
        Am. Ch. Donna of Edgebrook
    Easebourne Bellmaid
        Rakemakers Ringer
        Easebourne Sonnet

Lita of Chichester
    Stormer of Reynalton
        Hardway of Reynalton
        Minerva of Reynalton
    Mischief of Reynalton
        Ringer of Reynalton
        Minerva of Reynalton

Dual Ch. Easebourne Tarquin

Ch. Coral of
   Westsummerland

Tess of Synlew

Captain of Brighton
Blanche of Brighton

Hercules of
   Reynalton
Juno of Reynalton

WT Ch. Raycroft Jasmine

WT Ch. Raycroft Jailer	Easebourne Senator	Am. & Eng. Ch. Spotter of Littlebrook
		Easebourne Bellmaid
	Lita of Chichester	Stormer of Reynalton
		Mischief of Reynalton
Anna of Bratton-Tor	Turpin of Reynalton	Ledburn Carbine
		Georgina of Brighton
	Sarah of Bratton-Tor	Ch. Dasher of Brighton
		Bratton-Tor Crackshot

WT Ch. Buxhall Anna

Ch. Buccaneer of Brighton

Buxhall Velvet

Ch. Challenger of Brighton

Amber of Brighton

Dual Ch. Easebourne Tarquin

Buxhall Henrietta

Captain of Brighton
Blanche of Brighton

Westsummerland Montgomery of Bre-Mar-Har-Ros
Rumba of Brighton

Ch. Coral of Westsummerland
Tess of Synlew

Easebourne Bangle
Ch. Dasher of Brighton

WT Ch. Sanguine Abingerwood Tinsel
('Sanguine' had dreadful feet, paper thin and flat, but in spite of this was an excellent worker and won her second Working Trial Certificate in the record time of 22 minutes. Hunting ability is more important than conformation)

Abingerwood Nobleman	Abingerwood Barsheen Jason	Ch. Barsheen Goliath Ch. Barsheen Jewel
	Ch. Gala of Brighton	Ch. Dominator of Brighton Bouquet of Brighton
Garnet of Brighton	Ch. Dominator of Brighton	Captain of Brighton Ch. Challenger of Brighton
	Bouquet of Brighton	Amber of Brighton Rosette of Brighton

WT Ch. Sherlock Sea Urchin

	Am. Ch. Hull Downs Milk Ear Willie	Am. Ch. Wotan Am. Ch. Kaa of the Chase
Abingerwood Lime Tree Pendragon		
	Am. Ch. St Huberts Britamart	Am. Ch. Thor of Gunmar The Rings Nedda
	Ch. Appeline Hector of Westsummerland	Westsummerland Montgomery of Bre-Mar-Har-Ros Emily of Westsummerland
The Cherokee of Brighton		
	Delburn Blackie	Raycroft Actor Fantasia of Brighton

WT Ch. Gotwick Mettle
(Mettle won her first Working Trial Certificate at the exceptionally early age of 2 years 2 months, hunting at great speed on a leash, handled by her owner's 10-year-old sister Angela Seymour.)

Ch. The Cheyenne of Brighton	Ch. Appeline Hector of Westsummerland	Westsummerland Montgomery of Bre-Mar-Har-Ros
		Ch. Emily of Westsummerland
	Delburn Blackie	Raycroft Actor
		Fantasia of Brighton
Barsheen Onyx	Ch. Barsheen Nicholas	Ch. Barsheen Benedict
		Ch. Barsheen Jewel
	Ch. Barsheen Ruby	Ch. Appeline Hector of Westsummerland
		Ch. Barsheen Gem

WT Ch. Sanguine Saintly

Ch. The Cheyenne of Brighton

    Ch. Appeline Hector of Westsummerland

        Westsummerland Montgomery of Bre-Mar-Har-Ros

        Ch. Emily of Westsummerland

    Delburn Blackie

        Raycroft Actor

        Fantasia of Brighton

WT Ch. Sanguine Abingerwood Tinsel

    Abingerwood Nobleman

        Abingerwood Barsheen Jason

        Ch. Gala of Brighton

    Garnet of Brighton

        Ch. Dominator of Brighton

        Bouquet of Brighton

WT Ch. Heath Hill Vermouth
(Vermouth held all the cups shown here at the same period in 1971. They are (*left to right*): Brough Cup, Tremaric Cup, Williams Cup, Savernake Cup, (*front*) Ailesbury Bowl.)

	Raycroft Vandal	Raycroft Diver
Raycroft View		Raycroft Amber
	Buxhall Gaidheal Bashful	Easebourne Forager
		WT Ch. Buxhall Anna
	Barsheen Benjamin	Barsheen Benedict
Raycroft Ballard		Barsheen Ruby
	Gaidheal Anastasia	Raycroft Falcon
		WT Ch. Buxhall Anna

WT Ch. Sanguine Saturn

Raycroft View	Raycroft Vandal	Raycroft Diver Raycroft Amber
	Buxhall Gaidheal Bashful	Easebourne Forager WT Ch. Buxhall Anna
Wantsley Mermaid	Ch. Barsheen Zak	Ch. Kirk of Thunderdell Barsheen Nicola
	WT Ch. Gotwick Mettle	Ch. The Cheyenne of Brighton Barsheen Onyx

WT Ch. Rushton Rochester

Raycroft Rector	Sabden Royal	Barsheen Neil Sabden Juliana
	Raycroft Bargain	Raycroft Tipster Raycroft Bounty
Judston Juno	Pluto of Brighton	Ch. The Cheyenne of Brighton Kindly of Brighton
	Sabden Naomi	Rytow Thoughtful Sabden Juliana

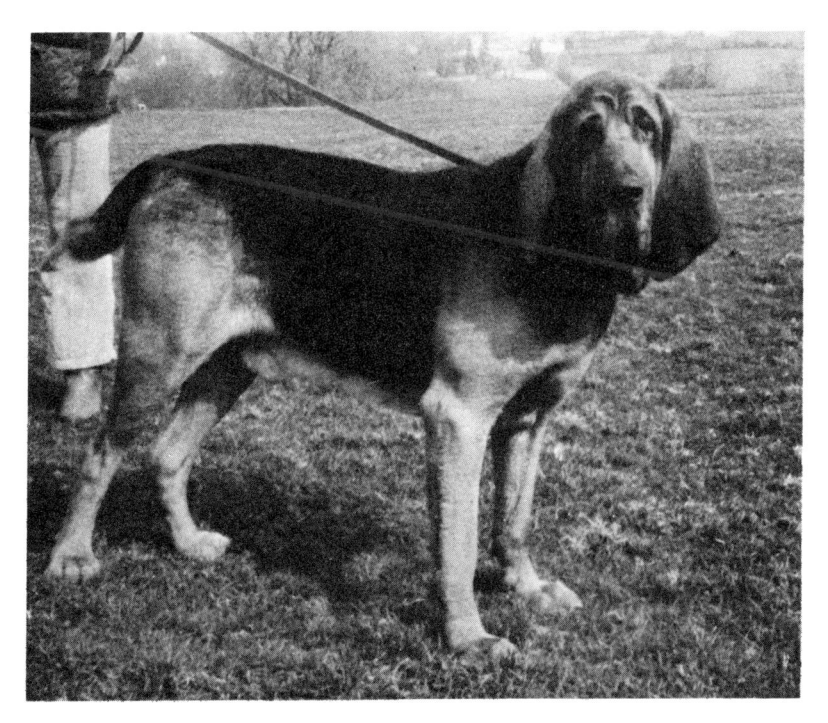

WT Ch. Penton Houdini

Perryhill Grimaldi

    Ch. Barsheen Zak

        Ch. Kirk of
        Thunderdell
        Barsheen Nicola

    Abingerwood Carla

        Abingerwood
        Limetree
        Pendragon
        Ch. Abingerwood
        Prudence

Barilla Lucia

    Barilla Barsheen
    Parthia

        Ch. Abingerwood
        Winged Pharoah
        Barsheen Ozannah
        de la Meutre
        d'Autrefois

    Barsheen Lucinda

        Ch. Barsheen
        Nicholas
        Ch. Barsheen Lucette

2
Acquiring and Training a Puppy

There are many people with a wealth of experience in the raising and training of bloodhound puppies and I have felt it useful to include one of these who has had many years' experience in breeding, showing and trialing.

I am therefore very grateful to Mrs Bobbie Edwards who has contributed this chapter and part of Chapter 4. Mrs Edwards is Hon. Secretary of the Bloodhound Club, Hon. Secretary of the Hound Association and Bloodhound Breed Representative to the Breed and Working Trial Kennel Club Liaison Councils.

'Why do You Want a Bloodhound?

If you covet a bloodhound as a status symbol, forget it and choose another breed instead. Bloodhounds are large, handsome creatures and will be much admired by your acquaintances. However, they have a number of undesirable traits which do not endear them to those who are not dedicated to the breed, and it is as well to find out as much as you can about them before deciding to own one. The breed clubs run welfare sections to help find homes for unwanted bloodhounds – frequently because breeders have not been sufficiently selective in the first place, and the homes have been completely unsuitable.

Disadvantages

They are very expensive to buy and to rear; they are very large, strong and rather clumsy and are not suitable for the old or frail;

they have an independent, wilful nature that is not easily trained for obedience and a tendency towards aggressiveness if not properly reared; their slow maturation and size leads to destructiveness for a seemingly endless period – bloodhounds and Chippendale furniture do not go together; they are very boisterous when young, particularly if underexercised, and need a great deal of exercise to keep fit and contented; they have a tendency towards various health problems, particularly bloat, eye, ear and skin infections, cancer, and have a comparatively short life span (some can live until ten or even eleven years of age, but on average six or seven is more likely); they are not for the houseproud, as, on top of a tendency to chew the furniture, they slobber over everything, particularly if heavily jowled, and their coat is surprisingly thick, causing drifts of hair when moulting, particularly if kept in a centrally heated house; they are basically pack animals, and need companionship, without which they can be very destructive and belligerent.

Bloodhound and litter (from *The Illustrated Sporting and Dramatic News*, 1884).

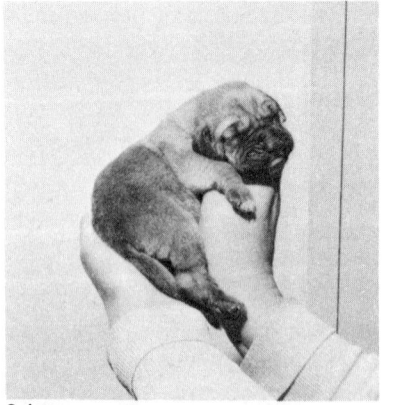

3 days

2½ weeks

4½ weeks

6½ weeks

8½ weeks

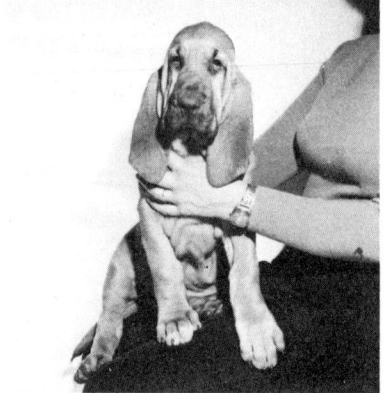

10½ weeks

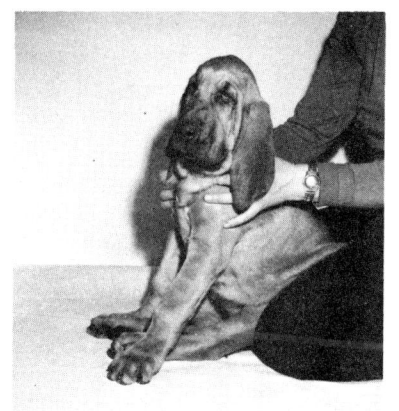

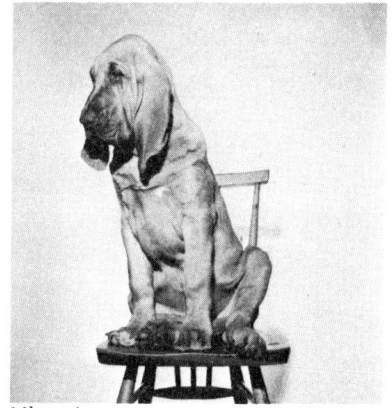

12½ weeks   14½ weeks

Bloodhound puppies grow extremely rapidly. This is Ch. Sanguine Saint.

Advantages

If reared properly, they have a delightful nature, with extreme affection for owner and family and toleration for strangers; they make excellent companions, fitting in well with family, children and other animals; they seldom fight; they are placid when there is nothing special happening, but enthusiastic for exercise or work; they have a wonderful sense of smell and a natural instinct for hunting, which alone makes the bloodhound worthwhile to a sporting owner. Anyone who enjoys watching hound work and does not have the opportunity to watch foxhounds, can have endless sport with a bloodhound. A single bloodhound can be as enthralling as a pack of hounds. They are truly three-dimensional animals, being companions, working hounds and show dogs, and the best combine all three properties to great advantage. Real bloodhound enthusiasts would not change to any other breed, as there is no other breed with their personality and purpose.

Is Your Home or Way of Life Suitable for a Bloodhound?

When you go to choose a puppy, you may find, to your surprise, that the breeder is assessing you as to your suitability. Conscientious breeders are very concerned that their puppies go to good homes and, whilst they are naturally anxious to effect a sale (the costs of rearing the dam and puppies being enormous), they would rather not sell if they think you are unsuitable in any way.

Bloodhounds are naturally gregarious so do not buy one if you are going to be away from home a lot and the puppy is to be left alone most of the day. Obviously you cannot be with it twenty-four hours a day, seven days a week, and it will be quite happy for short periods on its own, but unless there is another animal in the house for companionship it is unfair to expect it to live a solitary life. A bloodhound needs a suitable room in which to live, a fenced-in yard and a large space where it can be exercised freely, either common land or farmland. They are not suitable for small flats or in areas where dogs can only be exercised on a lead.

You must also have sufficient funds to give the hound what it needs in the way of food and care. They are large animals, growing from about $1\frac{1}{4}$ lb (0.5 kg) at birth to 100 lb (45 kg) at a year and it takes a lot of good food to achieve the necessary growth. Vaccinations and general veterinary attention are also very expensive, as is the replacement of furniture and treasures swallowed by the growing pup.

It is not advisable to keep a bloodhound outside in restricted surroundings unless one has very tolerant neighbours, as they can be rather noisy, sometimes waking early to herald the dawn in melodious tones.'

I remember the first occasion when one of our old dog hounds, Sanguine Sable, woke us and our neighbours in the early hours, dolefully baying at the moon. One neighbour telephoned to ask if our hound was all right or 'did it have croup?'

'A bloodhound usually fits in well with a household, but can be a problem if the sole responsibility of a parent with young children who does not have the time or freedom to exercise it properly. Whilst they are usually very patient with small children, they can be rather over-boisterous if encouraged to play rough games and can unintentionally cause hurt. Children must be taught not to disturb them whilst asleep, or tease them, particularly over food, as this can make them bad tempered. If suitably brought up together, however, a bloodhound will be completely trustworthy with children.

Ideally, you should be an active, energetic person, with plenty of time and energy to give the hound exercise, plenty of patience and firmness, combined with affection, with enough money to give it the necessities of life (but not so much that you live in such fine surroundings that the destruction of a priceless item will be a major disaster in your life). You should not be so houseproud that you cannot bear the slobber and hair that will accumulate. You should also not mind too much when the affectionate creature leans on you or puts its noble head on your knee, leaving behind a monstrous snail trail of slime. If the idea of this makes you shudder, a bloodhound is clearly not for you!

Before going to see any puppies, it would be a good idea to contact the breed club secretaries for the name and address of an owner living near you. This will enable you to meet their hound and 'talk bloodhounds' which will help convince you one way or the other as to whether you should buy this type of dog. Do make sure that you see many puppies from more than one kennel before you make your decision to buy one.

Choosing a Puppy

Decide why you want your hound and choose accordingly. If you particularly want a good show hound, do not be in too much of a hurry: you may be lucky and find what you want immediately or you may have to wait a considerable time. Go to as many shows as you can, join the breed clubs and read all available literature, and decide for yourself the points you are looking for and which kennel shows these points. Then book a puppy from the kennel, specifying that you want to exhibit it. Few good breeders in these circumstances will sell you a poor specimen, although of course early promise doesn't always produce a winner, and its future career will depend enormously upon you, but if you buy a mediocre puppy you have no chance of success at all. Do not necessarily expect a breeder to point out a puppy's faults,

WT Ch. Sanguine Saintly (*right*) with the Wuthering Cup awarded for the best dual purpose (show and working trial) hound of the year.

although it is to the breeder's advantage if only good stock bred by them appear in the show ring.

If, on the other hand, you are particularly interested in working your hound, show points are not so important, and you would be wise to make sure that your prospective puppy has good working antecedents. Whilst it is still instinctive in bloodhounds to use their noses, some strains have an added potential in this respect and it is noticeable that the top show kennels' affixes do not figure very largely in the working trials lists of competitors. This may, of course, be partly because show breeders tend to sell to exhibitors rather than to working owners. The hunting ability of a hound is, however, much more dependent upon the owner than the breeder and with good training any hound can become very good indeed. Care should be taken in choosing a hound for working that it is completely sound and built correctly, that its eyes are good and it has a bold, inquisitive nature.

If you merely want a bloodhound as a companion it is wise to choose carefully for temperament, and lack of physical disabilities that will affect a hound adversely in later life (such as entropion). The puppy should be bold and affectionate, and as far as possible similar to its prospective owners: a quiet hound for a quiet owner, a boisterous one for more jolly people, etc.

It is, of course, possible to combine all three functions and this is the ideal – a typical, beautiful specimen of the breed which hunts superlatively well and is a devoted companion – what more can you ask?

Your choice of puppy will depend upon your intentions for its later life: one that does not fit the breed Standard will still be good for working or as a companion, but puppies are not cheap to buy or to rear, so it is as well to choose carefully in the first place.

What to Look for in a Puppy

Study the breed Standard carefully. A puppy is a miniature, slightly caricatured copy of an adult, and a surprising amount of its future looks can be seen when only a few weeks old. Choose a puppy with a strong foreface, parallel skull, wide, deep chest, well

WT Ch. Buxhall Anna and a litter of puppies.

sloped shoulders, good strong hindquarters with good bend of stifle and hock, a long, well sprung ribcage, thick, sturdy legs and big, well knuckled feet. The head, in the very young, should be square, the length coming later, the wrinkle is very evident at this age and the ears long and carried low, although high set ears sometimes drop later. The stern should be strong and rather thick, sometimes it is too curly at eight weeks; if this is caused by lack of muscle underneath, it will probably straighten, but if it is a tight pig-like curl it will not improve. Study the eyes very carefully; these should be clear with the top eyelashes standing well away from the eyeball. Eyelashes pointing downwards and inwards indicate entropion in later life, and an operation will be necessary if the eye is not to be permanently damaged. Of great importance is the temperament; a puppy should be lively, playful, inquisitive and affectionate. It will probably be a little cautious in strange places or with strangers, but if nothing is done to frighten it, it should be inquisitive and approach and be friendly quite quickly. An over-timid puppy is likely to be nervous in later life and could become a fear-biter which, being unpredictable, can be dangerous in a large breed. Puppies reared in a busy household are usually much bolder than those reared in an outside kennel in isolated surroundings. They become conscious of their surroundings at about three weeks of age, and exposure to various stimuli from this age will affect their later life. The dam's temperament should be studied carefully, as there is no doubt that the puppy's temperament is partly hereditary, partly environmental and partly taught by their mother.

The biggest puppy in the litter will not necessarily turn out better than the smallest, although obviously it has a better start in life. Also puppies in a numerically big litter will take a little longer to gain size than those in a small litter.

Dog or Bitch?

Again, this is a matter of choice. Dogs are considerably bigger and heavier than bitches and are more difficult to handle. They are more independent and need firmer discipline, as their pack instincts are stronger and a weakly handled dog may decide to take over the pack leadership. They are usually considered to have more drive when working but are more easily distracted.

My own experience with dog hounds tends to contradict Bobbie's view that they are more easily distracted.'

'Bitches, on the other hand, are smaller, gentler, more easily disciplined and fit into a household easier. Their main disadvantage is their season, followed frequently by false pregnancies when they can become rather broody. Either sex can be delightful if reared properly or disastrous if not handled correctly, although it is usually dogs which have to be found new homes by the welfare sections of the breed clubs.

What Should you Pay?

This varies enormously from one breeder to another and the most expensive are not necessarily the best. It will also vary amongst the puppies in a litter depending upon the breeder's view as to their worth, so it is not possible even to give a rough estimate. If you think that too much is being charged, however, remember that at eight weeks the puppy is eating as much as its mother, and is also having expensive trace elements, vitamins and extra milk added to its diet. The breeder is having to keep the dam in a healthy condition, the stud fee has been paid, as have the veterinary fees and Kennel Club fees. It is also costing a great deal in sheer hard work to rear, and, if you are buying a puppy with good show and working prospects, it has cost its breeder a great deal to campaign its dam through a show or working career. All of this must be reflected in the puppy's price.

In breeder's language, 'pet' doesn't mean a companion, but a dog of less than show quality for one reason or another. If you only want a companion it is unfair to expect the breeder to drop his price because you 'just want a pet'.

If you buy the cheapest puppy in the litter you must not expect it to turn out the best looking, although with good rearing this can sometimes happen. A puppy sold as a 'pet' and later shown, if a poor specimen, does not do the breeder much good, even though he sold at a low price having been assured the animal would not be exhibited. Sometimes the breeder will mark the registration papers 'Not for Exhibition' to prevent this happening. Unfortunately, in the bloodhound breed this also prevents it from being entered for trials.

A breeder will quote a price for a puppy based on the puppy's present looks and temperament. If he sells a dog as a show potential, it is only that, not a guarantee, as most of its future development depends upon the buyer. It can be very disappointing for a breeder to see promising sturdy puppies turn into malformed weaklings because of the poor way in which they have been reared.

Virtually all breeders will have registered the puppies before sale, although the papers may not have been returned by the Kennel Club before the puppy is collected. The breeder should, however, give the prospective owner a pedigree for the puppy which shows its ancestors for four or five generations and which is signed by the breeder as accurate. This pedigree should show the Kennel Club registered numbers of both sire and dam. It is important that both parents are registered as it is not now possible to register any dog whose parents are unregistered.

If the puppy is to be exported, it will need an export pedigree and, in the case of a dog, a British veterinarian must sign the form to state that the dog is entire. In any case a puppy must be registered before leaving Britain, otherwise it will not be eligible for registration in the country of its adoption. A breeder will usually sell a puppy 'ex-kennels', all the extra costs of vaccination, or exporting, which can be quite considerable, being borne by the buyer.

Where Should it Live?

Because bloodhounds are gregarious creatures, I would not advise keeping one in a kennel outside, except at night or for short periods, unless it has a companion. A corner of the kitchen is ideal, in a large wooden box, slightly raised from the ground, about 2 ft (50 cm) by 3 ft (1 m) with sides $1-1\frac{1}{2}$ ft (25–45 cm) high (perhaps slightly larger for dog hounds). It can then be shut in the kitchen at night or when you are out, and should not be allowed to wander around the house getting into mischief. The household should recognise that this is its bed and it should be allowed to sleep undisturbed at all times.'

I tend to disagree with Bobbie on the use of the kitchen, not only because bloodhounds are such slobbery animals but also because they may break into food cupboards and feed themselves, thus running the risk of bloat which can be fatal.

'The box can be filled with a variety of things for bedding: blankets, cushions, etc., but it should be remembered that bedding harbours fleas, and so it should be washable or easily disposable. A strong cover filled with straw can be very good, or shredded newspaper makes a hygienic, disposable bed and has the advantage of drying the coat after exercise. Bloodhounds tend to develop hard bald patches on elbows and hocks if kept on a hard or rough surface.'

Whatever the material you use for the bedding, do be careful that it is entirely free from any harmful chemical agent.

'A puppy may howl at night a little to start with, but if it is basically happy, with plenty of companionship during the day and has its own box where it can sleep undisturbed when tired, it soon gets used to going to bed peacefully at night.

If possible, it is a good plan to have a yard separate from the family's garden, as a bloodhound can make a considerable mess. Some consider themselves to be good gardeners; digging up recently planted bushes or attempting to prune the roses. Another good idea is a hound door (like a cat door, only bigger) so that he can go in and out at will.

A puppy should be given its own toys when left on its own, such as a large marrow bone, stuffed sock, large carrot or potato, or a cardboard box to chew up. All valuables and edibles should be kept well out of reach, and children taught to shut doors and put their own toys away to avoid tragedies. If the puppy chews a forbidden article, it should be removed, the puppy growled at sternly and given its own toy immediately.

Feeding

It is virtually impossible to advise on feeding. This varies considerably from do-it-yourself feeding as is the practice in most kennels (fetching offal, sheeps' heads, cheeks and various of the cheaper meats from a slaughter house, boiling it, removing inedible bones and teeth, and mixing it with a home-made porridge-like concoction of flaked maize etc.) to feeding entirely on convenience foods specially made for dogs. The former is cheap but laborious, and requires careful balancing and correct additives; the latter expensive but readily available and the 'complete' foods are just that. The average dog is fed on a combination of the two.

Various points should be borne in mind, however, when feeding bloodhounds. A puppy grows extremely rapidly. At the period of maximum growth it may be gaining weight at a rate of over 5 lb (2 kg) a week. As you can imagine, this cannot be done on a poor diet, and if bloodhound puppies are not fed adequately, they will never develop the size and substance that they should. However, when fully grown, their needs diminish and, considering their size, they are not nearly as demanding in their requirements. It is the first year to eighteen months that need the most nourishment.

The meat fed, however, need not be of an expensive kind; scraps, offal, cheek etc. can be used and one can reduce costs considerably by making arrangements with local shops to buy cracked eggs, outdated baby milk, etc., and by buying in bulk.

Dogs are carnivores; people often wrongly think this means that they only eat meat, and sometimes feed dogs solely on meat, to the detriment of their health. Dogs in the wild eat the whole animal, muscles, fat, intestines and contents, bones, fur, skin and all. They need protein (found in meat, offal, fish, eggs, cheese etc.), fat (a much greater proportion of fat is needed than in humans), carbohydrates (biscuit, grain, bread etc.), roughage (vegetables and bones) and also vitamins and trace elements. Proteins, vitamins and trace elements (not forgetting calcium and Vitamin D which are essential for proper bone formation) are particularly important in the growing pup, and the proportion of these should be higher during the growth period than when adult.

Puppies at eight weeks need about as much protein as adults, and at their peak growing period should be given twice as much as the adult requirement. A rough guide would be 2 lb (1 kg) of meat daily for adults, and 4 lb (2 kg) daily for pups of nine to fifteen months. They should also get a pint of milk daily, although as some are allergic to cow's milk, this can be baby milk instead. Most breeders will give you a diet chart when you collect your puppy.

There are two schools of thought about puppy feeding – fat puppies or not so fat puppies. I personally believe that puppies should not be too fat as I consider that excess weight puts too much strain on immature bones and joints and leads to problems in later life. The puppy should be well covered, but the main aim should be to develop the bones and muscles, so I do not recommend a high carbohydrate diet for growing puppies.

Young puppies should be fed four or five times daily. As they grow older, their meals can be reduced to twice a day when adult. Because bloodhounds are prone to bloat, it is advisable always to feed twice a day, not once a day as usually recommended for dog feeding. The puppy should be given its meals at regular intervals, as much as it will eat, and what is left over should be removed as soon as the puppy shows lack of interest. It should *never* be left down for the puppy to peck at during the day. Bloodhound puppies frequently have poor appetites, particularly if kept singly, and if its food is always available it can get into the habit of nibbling at it without any real appetite or enthusiasm. If kept with other dogs, or if the food is removed as soon as it leaves it, the puppy soon learns that it will be unable to come back for more, and learns to eat properly.

Exercise

Again, there are two schools of thought – to exercise or not to exercise young puppies, which more or less fit in with the thoughts on feeding – fit or fat. My own feelings are that puppies may be exercised from a very young age, providing that the exercise is increased very gradually and that the puppy is never tired out. Free exercise, playing in a garden etc., is much better than being dragged about on a lead, although later on, road work is invaluable.

Building up the bones and muscles, not to mention heart and lungs, with gentle, carefully increased exercise will show itself in later years in properly developed shoulders and hindquarters. However, a word of caution – if your puppy is overweight and has not developed adequate muscles, too much exercise can cause strain in immature bones and joints and can cause the front legs to bend at the pasterns. Puppies should not be encouraged to jump down from high steps on to hard ground until they have built up their muscles properly. Children should not be allowed to overtire very young puppies.

House Training

Bloodhounds are naturally clean in their habits if allowed to be so, and learn quite quickly. The owner should take the new puppy outside immediately on waking and directly after meals, and praise it when it messes in the right place. It will soon learn, although it takes longer to learn control of the bladder, and puddles are inevitable. If it is not possible to arrange a hound door, put newspaper alongside the door and it will use that. The instinct is to mess as far from its bed as possible, so its box should be as far from the outer door as possible. There is no point in rubbing the puppy's nose in its mess or smacking it.

Adult hounds are sometimes dirty out of frustration or anger, when it may be done as a protest and there is always a reason for this behaviour, such as jealousy. Occasionally, this is a sign of illness, and the hound should be taken to the vet to find out the cause and so treat the problem.'

My wife Margaret and I have allowed our hounds into the house and it took us quite some time to realise that a message left on the floor, when decoded simply meant that a walk had been missed.

'General Training

When you get your new puppy home, it will naturally be alarmed by its strange surroundings and the journey home may have been quite frightening. If you can make friends whilst it is still on its home ground this will help. Reassure it, hold it and talk soothingly to it so that it regains its confidence. Puppies that have been reared in noisy households are more likely to settle quickly than those that have been raised in isolation, but if you treat it gently and considerately and talk to it, even a very timid puppy will gradually overcome its fears.

Keep it quietly at home for a few days (it must not, in any case, go out until it has had its vaccinations) and let it explore in its own time. Let it make the advances to the family and do not let children behave too boisterously near it until it is confident with them. If you have another dog or cat, introduce the new puppy with caution and do not leave them alone together until you are sure they are friendly. Most adult animals are very tolerant of the young, but some will be very jealous of the newcomer, so do not forget to fuss the older one as well as the new puppy. Bloodhounds thrive on affection and gain confidence very rapidly from their owner's calm behaviour, but can take a long time to get over an early traumatic experience that has really frightened them.

Bloodhound puppies chew everything they can get their teeth into, and it is best to keep valuables well out of reach. This behaviour, as with a human baby, is partly experimental and also because they are teething and require hard surfaces to bring their teeth through properly. The corner of the coffee table, for example, is ideal, being just the right height for a good meditative chew. The baby puppy is not being naughty, so do not smack him for this behaviour (not at least until he is much older and knows that it is wrong). As soon as he starts to chew a forbidden object, growl at him and give him his own toy – a marrow bone is ideal. It is likely he will soon learn.

Tearing things up is also highly enjoyable, and cardboard boxes and cartons can keep a puppy happy for a long time. As they get older, they chew because they are bored, so if he has to be alone, be careful to shut him up somewhere where he can do no harm and give him things to play with.

A puppy's first teeth are very sharp and he has no idea of the pain inflicted on fingers and ankles, but growling will teach him to be gentle (adult dogs do this to puppies). It is very easy to teach a hound bad table manners, and it is advisable never to feed a hound except from his own bowl at the proper times. Do not give scraps from the table or allow the children to feed him from their plates, or you will have a pathetic, apparently starved creature watching your every mouthful, with long threads of dribble hanging from his mouth – a sight guaranteed to make you lose your appetite. If you do not feed him from the table, he will quickly learn to leave you in peace for your meals.

Most bloodhounds readily take to car travel once their initial apprehension is overcome, particularly if this is associated with walks or hunting. If your local exercise area is on your doorstep and the only time the hound goes in the car it is to go to the vet, naturally he will be apprehensive. In this case it is a good idea to put him in the car and drive around for a short while before exercising him so that he associates the car with something pleasurable.

Bloodhounds are naturally rather possessive and tend to protect their food, beds and homes against strangers. It is well to stroke the new puppy whilst he is eating from the beginning so that he does not object to your being near his food. Stroking the puppy in his bed will also get him used to having his bedding changed. However, if he objects and, unless you want to make an issue of it, it is best to shut him out of his room while you change his bedding. Children should never touch the hound whilst he is asleep in his bed unless he has a very gentle nature, and he should never be teased with food. Even a gentle hound, if a child jumps on him whilst asleep, can turn and bite before he realises what is happening, although bloodhounds are usually very tolerant.

If you have more than one dog, it saves a lot of argument if each animal has its own place for its feeding bowl and they are always fed in the same place. Most bloodhounds, after puppyhood, prefer to sleep singly and not with other dogs, so separate beds are preferable to one big bed.

Bloodhounds tend to guard their cars and homes against stangers and it is a foolhardy person who would walk into an unoccupied car or house that contained a bloodhound. However, if the owner is with the animal and reassures it, most allow strangers to approach with no difficulty.

An otherwise good tempered hound can be spoilt quite easily by teasing or jeering. Beware particularly if you are out, and teenagers can taunt a hound through the fence.

It is very important to establish the new puppy's position in the family right from the beginning. A bloodhound is basically a pack animal, whose natural instincts are to a group. Anyone who has seen wolves in a zoo, or chickens in a yard will know that they have a definite 'pecking' order. Provided this is established properly, the whole pack lives in peace and there is no quarrelling. However, fighting breaks out when a younger or junior animal tries to dominate the one above it in the pack and, until the pecking order is again established, there will be quarrels to a greater or lesser degree depending upon how insistent the junior is, or how weak or powerful he thinks his superior is. This holds good for all the dog family, but the more sociable an animal is, the greater the pecking order (a hound is a pack animal; a terrier is not).

The bloodhound is a particularly social breed and can live in harmony with other dogs, people or animals and is only really happy in company. However, if a puppy is spoilt and allowed to have its own way all the time, as it gets older it will decide to lead the pack itself, in this case the pack being its owner and family. If you like to be dominated, of course, there would be no problem provided you do exactly as it wants you to! Most humans prefer to run their households their way, and the young bloodhound must be taught from an early age that you will stand no nonsense and any question of a take-over bid is definitely out. So establish the rules early and stick to them; it will only confuse a young animal if it does not know from day to day what it is, or is not allowed to do.

Any attempt at real aggression towards its owner must be met with instant domination. If it comes to a battle you must win at all costs, and sufficiently clearly that the hound knows there is no point in trying again. This may not happen if the young hound is properly disciplined, but the age at which they reach sexual maturity (nine to fifteen months) is the most likely time for this. It is at this stage that the breed clubs get cries for help to find the dog a good home, simply because their owners have spoilt them as puppies and are frightened when the hound shows the inevitable aggression.

I do not advocate hitting a bloodhound for normal offences –

Bloodhounds make excellent companions, fitting in well with families and children.
Timothy Lowe and Boravin Fusilier, Bloodhound Club trials, Yorkshire, autumn, 1979.

usually an angry voice is enough to make them apologise – but out and out aggression is something else and must be met with instant, complete domination. Shaking hard by the loose skin on the cheeks is good, holding one cheek tightly with one hand and hitting the side of the face with an open palm is also effective. There is no point in hitting their backsides (it will only hurt your hand) and a stick may cause real damage. A whip is useful as it stings and does not damage, but you seldom have one to hand, and the reaction from you must be as instantaneous as the bite of another dog.

You should continue the punishment until all the fight goes out of him, he puts his tail between his legs and rolls over in submission. Another growl from you for luck, then you make friends again. It is better to establish your dominance over the animal and turn it into a civilised member of the family than to have to get rid of it or put it down. Strangely enough after this has happened, the hound will be much more affectionate and respect you for having established your right to pack leadership.

This is the only occasion when a hound should be hit; usually a growling voice will be enough to stop him doing what he knows he should not, although a good shaking is understood by a puppy as this is the way that his mother would discipline him. Bloodhounds respond best to a tremendous amount of affection together with firmness; harsh treatment will make them cowed and perhaps treacherous.

Lead Training

Put a collar on the puppy well before you want to take him out on a lead, so that he can get used to it without other distractions. Most puppies do not mind wearing a collar at all. A slip collar is best, as their heads are narrow, necks thick and ears too low set to make an ordinary collar firm. If they are frightened on a road they can jump suddenly backwards and come out of an ordinary fixed collar. Because a chain collar will cut the coat and cause bald patches on the loose skin under the neck, a leather or nylon slip collar is best, the nylon one being very cheap and strong.

Teach the puppy to come when he is called and to follow you round the house and in the garden, and give him little titbits to encourage him. Then put the lead on and continue in the same way, calling and encouraging him with titbits. Not until he is entirely happy on the lead in the garden should you take him out.

He will probably be terrified of the traffic outside, so sit with him on the pavement, stroking him and talking to him until he regains his confidence. Lorries and motor bicycles are particularly frightening to a youngster. Try to start him in a quiet road and gradually introduce him to busy roads but, if he shows fear, remember to reassure him and do not just try to drag him along.

When he is confident, elementary training is necessary, walking to heel without pulling, coming when called, sitting to order and so on. Teach him not to pull on the lead, as he will grow very big and it is exhausting and unnecessary to be dragged along by a bloodhound. It is useful to go to training classes at about six months of age where he can learn normal dog behaviour and get used to meeting people and strange dogs. Most local canine societies run training classes and the police can usually give you information in your area. Some instructors are, of course, better than others, but bloodhounds respond reasonably well, if a trifle slowly, particularly if the emphasis is on praise. The police style of training seems to suit bloodhounds better than the very strict training used for obedience competition work.

Gain your puppy's confidence and teach him to come when he is called before he is allowed loose in a park or farmland. Bloodhounds are prone to finding interesting smells and tend to tear off after a good scent, absolutely oblivious to the owner's cries. Do not, therefore, let him off the lead anywhere near traffic, particularly at the beginning of a walk when he is very fresh and enthusiastic.

Some bloodhounds swim with enjoyment, but often need another dog to show them how to, or to overcome their natural reluctance. Puppies should never be allowed to chase farm stock, especially sheep, and should be trained at an early age to ignore them.

Training Your Puppy to Hunt Man

The basic instinct of the bloodhound is to use its nose to track its quarry which, for hundreds of years, has been man. This instinct has been fostered by careful breeding over countless generations, and although at the present time, dogs are bred, regrettably, for the show ring rather than for their working potential, the instinct is still very strong. If you have ever seen a young Border Collie trying to round up the members of its family whilst being taken for a walk, you will see how its in-built instinct works. In the same way, a tiny bloodhound puppy will instinctively, when put into a strange place, use its nose to find its way around. Training is largely a matter of harnessing and encouraging this instinct.

First Lessons

Early lessons must be made into an exciting game. Remember that the very young puppy must never become overtired or bored and so keep the lines short and hot, i.e. put the puppy on the scent only a short time after the track-layer has walked. Do not let your enthusiasm run away with you by testing him to see if he can do difficult lines too early, or if you must, make them short and be prepared to give him an easy one immediately afterwards to regain his enthusiasm, particularly if he failed to find the scent the first time. Remember always to finish on a note of success: if at any time a hound who is trying hard fails to find the scent, give him another very easy line so that he remains keen for another day.

This maxim holds good throughout his working life, the keynote of good training is success in finding his quarry, and even though he has made a complete hash of his line, it is always a good policy to take him to the runner at the end and preferably let him hunt in the last hundred paces or so. If, during his training, a hound has difficulty in working the line set for him, it is a good plan to revert to an easier line before tackling the difficult problem again, so that his confidence is maintained.

The first lessons are a matter of hide and seek with the owner. Really there is no age that is too young to start, providing the puppy is physically advanced enough and has had his vaccinations, although he can begin even earlier if your garden is big and rambling enough for hide and seek games. The very young puppy should start on very short lines, the older one can try longer ones,

Sanguine Sans Pareil demonstrates first steps in hunting!

but it is better to do several short lines in the initial stages rather than one long one, because then the puppy has the reward of finding his owner constantly repeated. If the puppy is really very young, you can wait until his attention is away from you, hide behind a bush and call him. When he finds you, praise him and give him a titbit. Repeat this several times, rewarding and praising him each time, but do not go on so long that he gets bored.

When the puppy is a little older, you will need a 'handler' to hold him while you hide. If possible, this person should be a stranger to the puppy, so that he wants to find you and not stay with the person holding him. At this stage, use a 'smeller'; a piece of clothing, handkerchief, sock or rag, that has been worn close to your skin for some time, so that it has become impregnated with your scent. Whilst the handler holds the puppy, put your smeller on the ground in front of him and walk away, calling him, and hide behind a bush. The handler should then take the puppy up to the smeller, holding the puppy's head up until he drops it on to the scent article. The handler then commands the puppy to start to hunt, using a particular phrase which you will always use in future lines when 'laying on' your hound, and releases the puppy. This command can be 'Hie seek', or really anything you care to use, but the words and tone of voice should always be the same so that the puppy will learn to associate the command with the action.

The handler should know exactly where you have walked, and should walk in your footsteps behind the puppy, encouraging him on. If the puppy does not put his nose down immediately, the handler should point at the ground in front of him and call, 'Try here' (or whatever words you choose for this command). When the puppy comes to you, he will be very pleased to find you and you should make a terrific fuss over him and congratulate him immensely – even if this first attempt has not really been very successful – and reward him with a titbit. Immediately repeat the performance and again two or three more times until the puppy knows what he is doing, and then rest him.

This lesson can be repeated later in the day, and every day if possible, remembering to make the whole thing very exciting and never so long that the puppy becomes bored. Do not worry if on the first few occasions the puppy does not use his nose to find you but tries to use his eyes, the main thing is that he understands that he is supposed to find you. If he persists on using his eyes, make the handler hold him so that he cannot see you walk away, and refrain from calling him so that he does not know in which direction to search; he will soon get the idea.

The first lessons should be on easy ground without other scents or obstacles as far as possible, and with few distractions. A deserted grass field is ideal, long grass tends to carry a good scent and if there have been no other humans or animals in the field, there will be no other scents to confuse the puppy. It may be that you have no such place for training, in which case find the quietest place that you can.

Sanguine Saga on the line during training.

More Complicated Lines

Once the puppy can do short, hot (fresh) lines, tracking his owner with confidence, complications can be introduced. These include tracking someone else, making the lines longer and colder, introducing turns and obstacles, crossed lines, stock and wildlife. Never introduce two complications at once, and it is good policy to revert to an otherwise easy line when introducing a new problem, so that the hound's enthusiasm will carry it over the difficulty easier. If he has difficulty in working out a problem, take him back one stage and regain his confidence before tackling it again.

When the puppy can hunt his owner efficiently, the owner should take over the handling and, I feel, should always hunt him in the future. If the puppy is jointly owned, of course, both owners will want to work him, but unless their commands and methods of working are similar, confusion can arise in the puppy's mind, and he may not develop his potential properly. So, on the whole, I would advise that only one person handles; although I do know of several instances of hounds being handled successfully by more

Bobbie Edwards lays the short line and calls Saga and Sanft from the smeller. Henry Edwards and Nick Sutcliffe are the handlers.

than one person, this is the exception rather than the rule. The puppy should first be asked to find someone he knows well, such as a member of the family, and gradually the lines should be laid by people he knows, progressing eventually to strangers.

The 'runner' (the track-layer is called the runner no matter the speed of his progress) should leave behind a smeller. The handler (now yourself) should take the puppy to the smeller and drop his head on to it with the special command. Then handle him as before, walking along the line of the runner and encouraging him on. The runner should make a great fuss of him when he is found and give him titbits, even though they may be ill-deserved the first few times.

Once the puppy is proficient at short, hot lines, both the length of the track and the 'coldness' (the time lapse before laying on) can be increased. It is best not to increase both at once, but perhaps to alternate a short, cold line one day with a long, hot one the next. It is a mistake always to hunt the same distance, as the hound will begin to lose interest if he does not find his runner after the expected mileage. Scenting conditions vary, however, not only with the time lapse but also with the weather, and while a hound can gallop on a two-hour-cold line one day, he may find it impossibly difficult to work the next day. If he has a particularly difficult track it is best to make sure that his next is easy and rewarding.

Reading and Casting

When introducing twists and turns in the line, the puppy will be inclined to overshoot the line and run on farther than the point where the runner turned. The handler should always follow on the line, being careful to remain far enough behind that he does not overshoot as well. He should then stand still and quietly whilst the puppy casts (circles round looking for the scent). Casting tends to be instinctive, but will be assisted if the handler remains at the spot where the hound lost the scent, so that the puppy works around him. It is essential to watch the puppy closely for any sign that he has found the scent. When he does, give him a little verbal

Because this was Sanguine Sanft's first effort at hunting, he did not have a proper harness and the lead is attached to the collar. A cheap harness for a growing puppy can be made from webbing until it is worthwhile getting a proper one. The handler here is Sue Sutcliffe.

encouragement but do not make the mistake of cheering him on too enthusiastically until you are really sure he is right.

If you always know exactly where the runner has walked you will quickly learn to 'read' your hound and recognise when he has picked up the scent. He will turn on it suddenly as he crosses it, his stern will 'feather' and he will suddenly look excited and busy. Some hounds will 'throw their tongue', 'speak' or, in layman's language, 'bay' when they hit off the line. Each hound hunts in a slightly different way and some are easier to read than others, but half the secret of good handling is to be able to recognise exactly what your hound is doing, at any time. It is a great mistake to cheer a hound on when he is wrong, or to rate him (scold him) when he is correct; one bad reaction on the handler's part can undo much useful training. Therefore, if in doubt, say nothing and leave it to the hound to work out for himself.

If the puppy, after trying hard for some time to regain the line, begins to lose confidence and looks to you for help, walk in the direction the runner actually went, saying 'Try here' (or similar words, spoken always in a particular tone of voice). The puppy will follow, pick up the line and carry it forward, and the handler should encourage him on with the voice.

As the puppy becomes more proficient, it is possible to encourage him to cast by an expansive wave of the arm in the direction required and the encouragement, 'Try on'. Bloodhounds are the only breed of scent hounds which will cast back, that is, circle back to the line to a point before the scent was lost, and work it out again, usually rather slowly this time.

Watch the hound closely while he is casting; if he cannot find the scent, it may be because he has not 'completed his cast' or covered the whole ground round the point where he lost it. He should cast in each area like a windscreen wiper, using the handler as the pivot, and making an ever-widening arc until the scent is regained. The handler can move his position once one part has been thoroughly searched so that the hound will cast in a different direction.

Handlers vary tremendously in the way they cast their hounds. Some try to make the hound sweep fresh ground almost immediately the scent is lost, by taking him into each section until the scent is found. I personally feel that the hound should be left alone to work it out for himself as far as possible, although he should never be allowed to become despondent. Too early casting on the handler's part tends to make him reliant upon the handler, and as soon as he loses the scent, he will look to you to put him right. This will not develop that dogged persistence which is the bloodhound's characteristic.

Often there is good reason why the hound has lost the scent, sometimes a sharp turn will throw him, in which case holding back a little will help to bring him back on to the line. Sometimes there is some sort of foil which obliterates the scent, such as cattle manure round a gateway. This is an instance when the handler can 'lift' the hound (take him off the line) and try him farther on beyond the foil. There is little point in persisting in an area where there clearly can be no scent.

Keep quiet and still when the hound is casting, as constant chatter and movement will distract him from his work, but be ready to encourage him when he hits off the line. If he loses confidence and looks to you for help, cast him forward on to fresh ground. If you notice that he has failed to complete his cast, take him over the omitted part and make him try there.

Obstacles

A young bloodhound must learn to negotiate obstacles, and it is a mistake to lift him over them when at exercise. Even very young puppies should be taught to cope with problems, and if the puppy is left behind when you climb a gate he will get very excited and try his best to follow you. Again, make the first obstacles very easy and gradually increase their difficulty. It is easier to teach a hound to negotiate obstacles when out for exercise than when working a line, and a difficult fence in the middle of a track may discourage him from hunting.

There is no reason why a fit hound should not be able to scale a five-barred gate, and if an obstacle is too high, he should try to find a way round, through, or under it. Puppies should be shown how to wriggle through obstacles and it is wise never to open a gate when out for a walk. Do not, however, encourage a very young puppy to jump down from high banks on to hard ground until his bones are formed, as he could damage his front legs. Wire, fences, gates, hedges, streams, ditches, etc. should all be within the capabilities of a fit bloodhound, and you should teach him at an early age to try to cope with them without help from you. It is no joke trying to lift an adult male bloodhound of 130 lb (59 kg) or so over a high wall, and it should not be necessary, except in very rare circumstances. Tight barbed wire over a sheep fence or fences and gates designed to keep deer out can be a problem where some assistance from the handler may be necessary.

Farm Stock and Wildlife

Young hounds must be taught to ignore farm stock and wildlife. If there is any tendency to chase after them, a roar of disapproval may do the trick. If he is persistent, put a very long leash, such as a clothes line or tracking leash on to his collar, let him run to the end of the leash and then suddenly jerk him over backwards with a very loud, angry cry of 'Riot'. Or a short piece of hosepipe flung like a boomerang, clipping him on the backside at the crucial moment is very salutary – if you are a good shot.

It is absolutely essential to train a young dog to ignore sheep. Farmers may well shoot on sight any dog caught worrying sheep, so it is in your own interest to make sure that your hound is safe and steady with them. To encourage owners to train their hounds with farm stock, both breed clubs insist upon hounds being hunted leashed until they hold a certificate to prove they are steady with stock, and they are not allowed further than the first stake in trials until they hold such a certificate. Moorland black-faced sheep are particularly attractive to hounds and there have been occasions at trials when hounds, used to ordinary farm sheep, have succumbed to the temptation, to the chagrin of their owners, and faced instant disqualification. Hounds are particularly likely to chase sheep when two or more are together, as then pack instincts play a part.

Deer are also a strong temptation. Whilst farmers are unlikely to shoot a hound chasing a deer, the hunt may go on for miles and last for hours. This is frustrating and worrying as you cannot be sure what will happen to the hound in your absence or what mischief he will get up to. Cattle on the other hand are seldom chased, except perhaps small calves. The boot is often on the other foot and cattle, particularly heifers and bullocks, are inclined to chase and attack hounds and can do real damage by trampling them or trapping them against a fence. It is as well, therefore, to accustom puppies to cattle by taking them into fields of milking cows, known to be quiet. If not frightened when young, a hound will learn to work right through a herd of cows.

Horses, particularly young ones, should be regarded with caution as they can be quite dangerous with hounds, and you would be advised to get out of a field of young horses smartly. If a line goes through frisky cattle or horses it is best to lift a young hound and cast him in the field beyond. Never disturb lambing sheep or, for that matter, cattle heavily in calf.

Varying Scenting Conditions

As well as livestock, young hounds should be accustomed to working in a variety of different terrains, as the scent changes considerably depending upon the sort of ground, and the weather conditions prevailing at the time. It is no good doing all your training on a fine day on lush meadowland and expecting the hound to be able to cope with a howling gale and plough. He must learn to cope with different conditions so that he can tackle them confidently.

Some types of ground seem to hold scent better than others. Usually where the vegetation is richest, the scent is best; poor soil does not carry a good scent. Thick vegetation carries scent well, a hard surface does not. Scent depends upon a variety of factors, besides the obvious one of the coldness of the line walked.

H. M. Budgett wrote a book entitled *Hunting by Scent* many years ago, using a bloodhound for his experiments and his long suffering wife to walk the lines. I particularly liked the part where his wife had to walk a line barefoot through snow to test one of his theories – such is enthusiasm! Nothing written since can dispute Budgett's theories, and there is no scientific instrument yet invented which is anywhere near as sensitive as a bloodhound's nose, so scent is still a fascinating and little understood subject.

There are differences of opinion as to exactly what a bloodhound is following when it hunts a person, as the track may be composed of a collection of different factors. The personal scent of each person seems to be as individual as a fingerprint and is composed of his natural body odour mixed with the smell of his clothing, which is affected by his occupation (such as coal dust on a coalmerchant), his personal habits, smells of soap, foods consumed, his age, race and many other factors which affect his personal scent. This individual scent is mixed with the scent formed by the disturbance of the ground, with the crushing of vegetation, insects, etc. There is also the factor of ground scent and wind scent. Some of the scent remains actually round the footsteps of the runner, some is blown like smoke downwind, sometimes a considerable distance, to settle against a barrier such as a thick hedge. Sometimes the scent stays close to the ground, sometimes it appears to rise from the ground and hang above it like mist. When this happens the hound will hunt with head up, and he is referred to as hunting a breast-high scent.

It would seem likely that the personal scent of the individual tends to evaporate as time goes on, whereas, to a certain extent, the ground disturbance scent gets stronger as damaged wildlife decays. Probably the scent the hound is following is a combination of these factors. These factors are in turn also influenced by the type of soil, the amount of vegetation, the wind speed and direction, temperature, humidity, chemical fertilisers, recent disturbance of the soil and a host of determining factors. Usually where the ground is warmer than the air the scent will be good, but poor if the air is warmer or the same temperature as the ground. Whatever the hound is using to find his quarry is surmise on our part, but it is nevertheless affected by conditions, and hounds should be trained as far as possible in varying terrain and weather.

Strong winds appear to confuse young hounds most, particularly a following wind or a strong cross-wind. They must be trained to come up to the wind, otherwise, because they find patches of blown scent, they tend to drift downwind. More experienced hounds will hug the ground scent closely if the wind is particularly strong, but youngsters must learn that the scent is better actually on the line, and the handler can encourage the hound to stay close by keeping slightly upwind of the track himself.

Crossed Lines

When a young hound is proficient in hunting a stranger over reasonably varied country, try him on a crossed line where another person has walked over the track laid by the runner. A much hotter track may tempt the hound to change (take the scent of the later walker). He is unlikely to change on to a colder (less recent) line as the scent will probably be weaker than the runner's. There are two ways of testing his reaction to a crossed line: either you can ask someone to walk deliberately across the line immediately before laying on, or you can work across a busy footpath. If the hound runs up the fresh track, he should be rated and brought back to the crossing, shown the smeller again and encouraged in the right direction. It is acceptable for him to check the fresh track, provided that he comes back to the correct one by himself. This shows you that the hound knows what he is doing, is aware of the fresh track, but is rejecting it. A properly trained hound should never change, and this is a very important part of the training of the youngster.

When the hound can cope confidently with a crossed line, you can try him on a diverging line. That is, two or more people walk together from the start and split up after a couple of hundred yards. It is important that the smeller left by the actual runner should be uncontaminated by any other person's scent, and the other person should initially be not too well known to the hound. Have the point where the tracks diverge well marked so that you can correct the hound if he is wrong. Eventually a hound should be able to follow the scent of a stranger without changing, even when a member of his own family has crossed the line; clearly this will need quite a lot of training.

The handler, Bob Maddox, gives Brighton's Noble Manner ('Luke') the smeller impregnated with the runner's scent.

Laying On

If your hound is to be used to find real lost persons, of course, a smeller will not always be available, although in a surprising number of cases a piece of clothing can be fetched, and it is definitely a good policy to have a smeller whenever possible. Failing this, the hound will have to be laid on in a place where the person is known to have walked – the ground beside a car, the flowerbed below a window where a burglar has entered etc. There is always the possibility, though, that someone else may have been there, and it is difficult to make this foolproof without a smeller. It is a good idea to practise lines where there is no smeller, but these should be started in ground which is, as far as possible, clean of other scents.

The hound should not always be laid on in the same direction as the runner walked, as he may get used to rushing off in a straight line without properly working the scent. Sometimes the line should be approached at right-angles; this will encourage him to cast properly at the beginning of the line.

Harnesses and Leashes

Very impetuous hounds are best worked in harness, so that their speed can be controlled until they have settled on the line. If desired, the leash can then be unclipped from the harness and the hound hunted free. The harness should only be put on directly before laying on, so that the hound comes to associate the harness with work.

A harness for a growing puppy can be made from webbing stitched in a figure of eight, with a buckled opening on the girth and a D-ring stitched to the cross-over point behind the shoulders. When more or less full grown, a proper harness can be made, either in leather, or, as is used more nowadays, in nylon webbing. This has the advantage of being impervious to water and mud, but can cut into the hound particularly at the elbows unless it is well fitting.

The tracking leash should be about 10 yd (10 m) long and should be light and strong with a clip on one end and a loop on the other. The leash should be kept out of the way of the hound and held high, particularly when casting, with the surplus gathered in so that it does not trip him or tangle in his legs, but it should be paid out so that he has the full range of the leash to work freely. Handling a hound on a leash is quite an art, particularly in close country. If he is pulled up too suddenly it can throw him off balance and upset his concentration and, because the leash is an encumbrance, the hound will generally require more encouragement than one worked free. The leash should never be attached to the hound's collar when working as this will tend to bring his head up and interfere with his work. He should be taken up to the smeller on the collar and the leash transferred to the harness when laying on.

There is some controversy over whether to hunt a hound in harness or not. A harness is, of course, the only way to handle a hound when looking for a genuinely lost person, unless the scent is so poor that it is easy to keep up with him. There is obviously no point in the hound finding his quarry if you are not with him. The proper use of a harness and leash can be very good when training a hound, especially if he has developed bad faults. He can be stopped physically, rated and laid on again if he has changed, rioted or committed any other offence. My first hound, trained initially very badly, threw me into despair on many occasions by flying off down a path for half a mile or so, oblivious to shouts, until she caught up with the picnickers she had found more interesting than her runner! I would bring her back, me furious and her unrepentant, to where I thought the line was, and try to put her on again – a time-consuming and frustrating operation! On a leash, however, she would not have been able to get away, I could have rated her immediately and laid her on straight away, while the change of scent was still in her mind. I later trained her in a harness, and whilst this hound turned out to be an excellent tracker, I could never really trust her to stick to the correct scent as she had not learnt this vital lesson while young. Her daughter, also a working trial champion, was trained largely in harness, learnt this and other important lessons early and was absolutely reliable.

If you do not start training until the puppy can run faster than you can, a harness can be useful to keep him under control until he has learnt the rules of the game. A hound in harness is under the control of the handler at all times, and can be taught to work at a speed that suits the owner. It helps to settle an overenthusiastic hound down on its line, and he can be released if desired when he has steadied up. But handling a long leash is a tricky business, especially in close country where a hound, when casting, can tangle you up in the bushes like a kitten with a ball of wool. A young hound, hunting enthusiastically but erratically, can also pull you off your feet with no difficulty and it is much easier to misdirect a hound if he is on a leash.

On the other hand, when hunting free, the hound has complete freedom to cast on his own and is not so dependent upon his handler for working out the line, and can move at the speed he desires, depending upon the scenting conditions. However, he is much more likely to run wild and is less likely to know immediately that he is expected to work, than when the harness is brought out.

Know the Route of the Line

When training, it is important always to know where the line goes. It can be helpful if the runner leaves clues *en route* – scrape marks across paths, markers in the form of bright pieces of wool, small pegs etc. – to show where he has been. These must be collected when finished, as they are unsightly and confusing if you want to track in the same area on another day. Beware of too many markers unless they are placed high up, as hounds have been known to look for them and ignore the line.

When you are reasonably confident of your hound's capabilities, it is a good plan to have a line laid which you only know in parts – a few definite landmarks and the finish. In this way you can learn to be reliant upon the hound but, if something goes wrong and the hound cannot work it out for himself, you can take him to the next landmark and cast him there. If you have enough helpers, someone who knows the line can accompany you, only telling you the direction if the hound cannot find it himself. This is useful practice for trials.

Remember though, whilst training, that runners do not always go the way they are supposed to – they misunderstand directions, are poor map readers or just simply forget their instructions. If in doubt, it is a good maxim always to trust your hound; he knows, because he is the one who has the nose, where the line actually goes. There have been innumerable occasions at trials when handlers have been observed pulling their hounds off the line, much to the mirth of the spectators who have the advantage of knowing where the runner went.

I remember one occasion when a very fast hound in a Senior Stake took what appeared to be – according to the judge's map – a wrong turning, and came to a very high deer gate. She put her paws up and insisted that the judge should open it; jumping up and bellowing in a very positive manner. Although the map showed this to be wrong, the hound was so persistent and the handler left so far behind, that the judge opened the gate. The hound sped through and found her runner in a very short time. He was very relieved to be discovered as he had been completely lost for some hours.

It is important whilst training that the hound should find its quarry eventually and you can only ensure this if you know where he is! More important, particularly with your first bloodhound, is that by always knowing exactly where the runner has walked, you will learn to read your hound. This is really the secret of good handling and, in the long run, good work by your hound. If you cheer him on when he is right and rate him when he is wrong, he will gain confidence in you and in his own work, and learn to stick to the scent he has been asked to find. There is nothing more discouraging to a hound of any age than to be pulled off the scent because the handler thinks – wrongly – that the runner has gone in a different direction. This is guaranteed to confuse him and will undo all the work you have achieved together. When the hound is being used either for a real job or is competing at working trials, of course, you will not know where the scent is and will have to rely on your hound's nose to tell you. If you have both trained together, you should have no difficulty, although, rather like the learner driver who on completing his test suddenly finds himself without the prop of an instructor, it is rather unnerving until you are used to it.

Identification

An important part of training for working trials is the identification of the runner at the end of the line. In the Senior Stake, the coveted Kennel Club Tracking Certificate for Bloodhounds will be withheld if the hound fails to identify, and in the other stakes this point is taken into account. The hound must pick out the runner from a small group and positively show the judge that this is the person whose scent he has been following. This can be done in many ways, the classic method being to put his paws on the runner's shoulder. However, this is seldom seen, partly because, on the whole, owners do not train their hounds well in this respect, and partly because they do not want their hounds to jump at people. Whilst it is a good thing at trials, it is irritating if a housedog insists upon jumping all over your visitors, who seldom find it even faintly amusing. There are other quite adequate ways in which a hound can identify his runner, such as licking a hand, waving the stern, jumping up and down, fixing him with a stare, speaking etc. It is best to foster whatever method a puppy uses naturally. This may sound complicated but really, if titbits and loads of praise have been given to the young hound throughout his training by the runner, he will come up to him keenly. The runner should wait until the hound has identified him before giving him his titbit, and he will be the more keen to make himself noticed if he is waiting for a reward.

Finally, do not forget that the hound must always have boundless enthusiasm for his work. Never let him get stale and do not push him beyond his capabilities. It is better to have a young hound with faults than one that is fault free but listless in his work. The faults can be ironed out as he gets older and steadier, but if he does not have drive when young, he will never develop it in later life. Be careful not to extinguish this keenness by overambitious training.'

3
The Standard – Function, Fault or Fancy

It is not my intention to dwell too much on the subject of showing hounds, but I feel that I must make some comment on the points observed when visiting shows.

It appears to me that the Bloodhound Standard is a much misunderstood, or worse still, a wilfully neglected element in the show ring. This Standard was set down by two nineteenth-century experts who were unquestionably great authorities of their day – Edwin Brough and Dr Sidney Turner. Their vast experience and knowledge of the breed was gained through extensive study and by working hounds for many years in the hunting field, and the Standard therefore gives due consideration to features aiding scenting ability and general fitness, whilst preserving the breed's essential character stamped on it over the centuries. The breed eventually evolved to this Standard and has been altered only marginally by the Breed Societies in the past few years (see page 81).

However, whether the hounds seen in the show ring conform to the Standard, is quite another matter. As one who believes that function plays the largest and most important part in deciding the look of any animal and that aesthetics should play a subordinate role, I must confess that I have serious misgivings about many decisions that are made in the show ring today. I have seen hounds clearly oversized, heavily boned and well covered with fatty tissue rather than muscle, winning awards in the show ring.

Careful cosmetics and handling can conceal a great deal from an inexperienced judge and many of those who show are very adept at hiding the faults.

A fairly typical comment heard from competitors is 'I don't know what is being judged today, wide heads or narrow heads... I can't understand what the judge is looking for'. Many judges seem to ignore the hindquarters of the animal entirely, and I have seen hounds with the most appalling straight stifle ('knee' joint) and minimal muscle for propelling power being awarded Championship Certificates.

It is a fact that many show hounds, straight stifle or not, are muscularly underdeveloped and it is my opinion that all show specimens should be in a fit condition if a high standard is to be maintained. Awards should be withheld if hounds fail to reach this quality.

Major Problems

Hip Displasia

Hip displasia has become a major problem with many breeds of dog, and bloodhounds are certainly prone to this disabling fault. Some people advocate the examination of all breeding stock by X-ray so that faults can be recognised before breeding is allowed to take place. However, there is much controversy surrounding this subject; many qualified people consider this to be a recipe for disaster. The very action of irradiating that particular area of the anatomy as a matter of course when the hounds are not clinically ill, could well do considerable harm in the long run through the mutation of genes, not to mention the risks involved in giving a general anaesthetic.

It would be far better to understand and observe hounds with good hindquarters and movement and only breed from those specimens. This is where the judge in the show ring has a responsible job to carry out and if that were done, it would do much to combat an extremely bad feature in the breed.

Size

Size over the accepted Standard weight and height is another commonly seen major fault. The Kennel Club Standard clearly states that in reference to height, there are agreed terms which should be adhered to; for example the Standard states that an adult dog hound should measure between 25 in. (63·5 cm) and 27 in. (68·5 cm), 'the greater to be preferred'. In other words, any measurement between 25 and 27 in. is permissible, but a hound of 27 in. is preferred. This implies that a hound of 28 in. (71 cm) is not as good as a shorter one within the Standard. I wish that judges would apply this rule, since most of the hounds winning awards today are much above this accepted height, which results in less agility in the hunting field. I think that it would be a good idea for the judge to take a measuring rod into the ring, as is done when horses are judged. It might cause a few red faces, but it would help to promote the official Standard once again.

Wrinkle and Bad Eyes

Another problem I am concerned about is that of an overabundant supply of wrinkle. I am the first to appreciate that the overexaggerated, wrinkled caricature of the bloodhound is amusing to behold; however, whim or fancy is not reason enough to accept it to the detriment of the hound's health. Neither is it the correct standard according to the official records.

There are some who say that the abundant supply of wrinkle helps the hound when in its natural environment by protecting its eyes and body so that it can easily barge through thorns and thickets. This is true to a limited extent and some loose skin protecting the eye is a valuable asset. However, too much wrinkle does more harm than good and almost certainly leads to bad eyesight and possibly even entropion and blindness. Entropion is the condition where the eyelids may be inverted or turned in, causing the lashes to rub against the eye surface; as opposed to ectropion where the eyelashes turn out. Needless to say, other breeds of hunting hounds without wrinkle manage, on the whole,

Sanguine Sally – in my opinion an example of a functional, alert hound.

to manoeuvre through thickets and fences, over country without difficulty or injury.

It is just not true that bloodhounds rely totally on their nose and scent without using their eyes. A hound which can see well is usually an alert hound. I am not suggesting that they require the eyesight of a gaze hound, but I am saying that to see well makes life much more pleasurable and interesting and is especially useful to them when working a scent over country. For example, on reaching an impenetrable hedge or high wall, an experienced hound will search for a way round or over the obstacle, which may mean that he will have to veer over 20 or 30 paces off the scent to find an opening or crossing before returning to the scent. Good eyesight makes this a far easier task and saves considerable time.

Having owned both hounds that could see well and those that could not, I speak from personal experience when I say that the differences between them were easily discernible. Those which were poorly sighted could be spotted often standing or sitting unable to see what was going on, retreating into their shells, oblivious to anything visually happening around them. A favourite pose adopted by these hounds was that stance I remember used by the old milk-float horse, suspended between the shafts, appearing blinkered and bored, back sunk in a somewhat relaxed and disconcerting fashion.

In contrast, the hounds with less wrinkle and better eyesight, were never seen in that pose. They were alert to everything that went on around them and responded accordingly.

It is always interesting to note whether a hound in the show ring has the problem of discharge from the eyes. Even if this has been carefully cleaned by the owner a stain will remain where weeping has occurred. There is only one diagnosis for this problem – bad eyes. Again, my comment is that if only hounds with good eyes were used for breeding, much of this problem would disappear. It is really the responsibility of breeders to bear this in mind.

Lip

Too much lip is a disadvantage in that the hound continually dribbles. Too little lip is considered bad aesthetically, but at the same time dismisses many salivary problems. There are those who claim that great abundance of lip is an aid to scenting. Frankly, I find this suspect, since I have hunted hounds which could be said to be a little under-lipped, but which have proved to have exceptional working ability.

Bloat

Most bloodhounds in their present form are prone towards bloat (gastric torsion). This is a particularly unpleasant and often fatal malady, causing the hound considerable pain. The hound 'blows up' as a sheep sometimes will and although temporary relief can be given in the same way as given to sheep, a hound nearly always dies unless immediate veterinary treatment is given. Eric Furness of Chesterfield, Master of the Peak Bloodhounds, largely eliminated bloat from his kennels by outcrossing the pure bloodhound with the Dumfriesshire foxhound.

Edwin Brough recommended that an outcross should be introduced every five years. There was no specific suggestion of the form this should take, but I believe the present Dumfriesshire foxhounds would have impressed him if he could see them today.

Again, it is probably wise to breed only from hounds that are free from bloat.

Points System in the Show Ring

It is difficult to judge one hound in the show ring by comparison with another. If both answer the required quality against the Standard, the decision will boil down to one of personal choice. However, as it happens, most hounds are dissimilar enough to make this choice less of a problem than would at first appear, many of them being less than ideal in one respect or another.

I have heard arguments for and against the use of a points system in judging. The major problem is one of administration, because there are too many features to keep track of. However, although it may be a laborious process to carry out, it would compel a judge to look more than head deep and force an overall consideration of the animal. I feel sure that this would help to sort out not only the hounds but also the judges.

If the principle of using a plus points system is correct but laborious, perhaps it may be worth considering a *faults* system as an alternative. It is expected that most hounds which are entered in a show, at least approximate to the Standard. Therefore, it might be useful to have a maximum number of 'fault' points which, when exceeded, would mean automatic elimination of the hound. Because a normal show hound would be expected to have more features correct than incorrect, a faults system would involve fewer points to add up and would therefore be easier to administrate in the ring than a plus points system.

Here is an example which might be considered for calculating the faults in a hound. The number of points allocated to each feature is fairly arbitrary at this stage.

Penalty points incurred for bad formation

		Hound 1	Hound 2	Hound 3	Hound 4
Head & Skull	5				
Mouth	3				
Eyes	5				
Ears	3				
Neck	3				
Forequarters	5				
Hindquarters	5				
Feet	3				
Tail	3				
Colour	2				
Weight	5				
Size	5				
Movement	7				
Total					

If a hound does not incur any penalty points, then he clearly wins, providing no other hound matches this score. This result holds, even if the judge prefers another hound for some reason. Only if there is more than one hound achieving the same score, does the judge have freedom to express a personal preference. The idea behind this is not to simply bring judging to the level of simple arithmetic, but to ensure that certain standards are upheld and to prevent emotional opinions overriding basic requirements. This procedure would naturally take a little longer than the present system but, for the sake of the breed, would be well worth the extra time and inconvenience.

We should always remember that although hounds are judged against each other, more importantly, they are judged against the Standard. I have seen hounds highly placed in shows that really had no right to be there at all. An indictment of the present system is that if you take your hound to enough shows it is possible to chalk up a number of first or second places by entering competitions with only one or two entries in the class. This builds up the status of your hound without any basis of merit or quality and in this way you can gain success by default on the part of others. A more careful study of the Standard will help to overcome such quirks in the system. If this action results in a great deal of wailing and gnashing of teeth from owners and breeders, then the only other thing to do is to change the Standard – perish the thought!

The Standard

The present official Kennel Club of Great Britain Standard is that defined by Edwin Brough and Dr Sidney Turner at the turn of the century with marginal alterations by the two breed societies in 1964.

I have also included the American Kennel Club Standard which differs slightly from the British version.

The Official Kennel Club of Great Britain Standard for the Bloodhound, 1979

Characteristics: The Bloodhound possesses in a most marked degree every point and characteristic of those dogs which hunt together by scent (Sagaces). He is very powerful and stands over more ground than is usual with hound of other breeds. The skin is thin and extremely loose, this being especially noticeable about the head and neck, where it hangs in deep folds. In temperament he is affectionate, neither quarrelsome with companions nor with other dogs. His nature is somewhat reserved and sensitive.

General Appearance: The expression is noble and dignified and characterised by solemnity, wisdom and power. The gait is elastic, swinging and free; the stern being carried high scimitar fashion.

Head and Skull: The head is narrow in proportion to its length and long in proportion to the body, tapering but slightly from the temples to the muzzle, thus (when viewed from above and in front) having the appearance of being flattened at the sides and of being nearly equal in width throughout its entire length. In profile the upper outline of the skull is nearly in the same plane as that of the foreface. The length from the end of the nose to stop (midway between the eyes) should not be less than that from stop to back of occipital protuberance (peak). The entire length of head from the posterior part of the occipital protuberance to the end of the muzzle should be 12 inches [30 cm] or more in dogs and 11 inches [28 cm] or more in bitches. The skull is long and narrow, with the occipital peak very pronounced. The brows are not prominent although owing to the deep-set eyes they may have that appearance. The foreface is long, deep and of even width throughout, with square outline when seen in profile. The head is furnished with an amount of loose skin, which in nearly every position appears super-abundant, but more particularly so when the head is carried low; the skin then falls into loose, pendulous ridges and folds, especially over the forehead and sides of the face. The nostrils are large and open. In front the lips fall squarely, making a right-angle with the upper line of the foreface; whilst behind they form deep, hanging flews, and being continued into the pendant folds of loose skin about the neck, constitute the dewlap, which is very pronounced. These characters are found, though in a less degree, in the bitch.

Eyes: The eyes are deeply sunk in the orbits, the lids assuming a lozenge or diamond shape, in consequence of the lower lids being dragged down and everted by the heavy flews. The eyes correspond with the general tone of colour of the animal, varying from deep hazel to yellow. The hazel colour is, however, to be preferred, although very seldom seen in the red and tan hounds.

Ears: The ears are thin and soft to the touch, extremely long, set very low, and fall in graceful folds, the lower parts curling inwards and backwards.

Neck: Should be long.

Forequarters: The shoulders muscular and well sloped backwards. The forelegs are straight and large in bone, with elbows squarely set.

Hindquarters: The thighs and second thighs (gaskins) are very muscular, the hocks well bent and let down and squarely set.

Feet: Should be strong and well knuckled up.

Body: The ribs are well sprung and the chest well let down between the forelegs forming a deep keel. The back and loins are strong, the latter deep and slightly arched.

Tail: The stern is long and thick tapering to a point, set on high with a moderate amount of hair underneath. It should be carried scimitar fashion, but not curled over the back or corkscrew at any time.

Colour: The colours are black and tan, liver and tan (red and tan) and red. The darker colours being sometimes interspersed with lighter or badger-coloured hair and sometimes flecked with white. A small amount of white is permissible on chest, feet and tip of stern.

Weight and Size: The mean average height of adult dogs is 26 inches [66 cm] and of bitches 24 inches [61 cm]. Dogs usually vary from 25 inches [63·5 cm] to 27 inches [68·5 cm], and bitches from 23 inches [58·5 cm] to 25 inches [63·5 cm]. The mean average weight of adult dogs in fair condition is 90 lb [41 kg], and of adult bitches 80 lb [36 kg]. Dogs attain the weight of 110 lb [50 kg], and bitches 100 lb [45 kg]. Hounds of the maximum height and weight are to be preferred providing always that quality, proportion and balance combine.

Note: Male animals should have two apparently normal testicles fully descended into the scrotum.

Official American Standard

General Character: The Bloodhound possesses, in a most marked degree, every point and characteristic of those dogs which hunt together by scent (Sagaces). He is very powerful and stands over more ground than is usual with hounds of other breeds. The skin is thin to the touch and extremely loose; this being more especially about the head and neck, where it hangs in deep folds.

Height: The mean average height of adult dogs is 26 inches [66 cm], and adult bitches 24 inches [61 cm]. Dogs usually vary from 25 inches [63·5 cm] to 27 inches [68·5 cm], and bitches from 23 to 25 inches [58·5 to 63·5 cm]; but in either case, the greater height is to be preferred, provided that character and quality are also combined.

Weight: The mean average weight of adult dogs, in fair condition, is 90 lb [41 kg], and of adult bitches 80 lb [36 kg]. Dogs attain the weight of 110 lb [50 kg], bitches 100 lb [45 kg]. The greater weight to be preferred, provided (as in the case of height) that quality and proportion are also combined.

Expression: The expression is noble and dignified, and characterised by solemnity, wisdom and power.

Temperament: In temperament he is extremely affectionate, neither quarrelsome with companions nor with other dogs. His nature is somewhat shy, and equally sensitive to kindness or correction by his master.

Head: The head is narrow in proportion to its length, and long in proportion to the body, tapering but slightly from the temples to the end of the muzzle, thus (when viewed from above and in front) having the appearance of being flattened at the sides and of being nearly equal in width throughout its entire length. In profile the upper outline of the skull is nearly in the same plane as that of the foreface. The length from end of nose to stop (midway between the eyes) should be not less than that from stop to back of occipital protuberance (peak). The entire length of head from the posterior part of the occipital protuberance to the end of the muzzle should be 12 inches [30 cm] or more in dogs, and 11 inches [28 cm] or more in bitches.

Skull: The skull is long and narrow, with the occipital peak very pronounced. The brows are not prominent although, owing to the deep-set eyes, they may have that appearance.

Foreface: The foreface is long, deep, and of even width throughout, with square outline when seen in profile.

Eyes: The eyes are deeply sunk in the orbits, the lids assuming a lozenge or diamond shape, in consequence of the lower lids being dragged down and everted by the heavy flews. The eyes correspond with the general tone of colour of the animal, varying from deep hazel to yellow. The hazel colour is, however, to be preferred although very seldom seen in red-and-tan hounds.

Ears: The ears are thin and soft to the touch, extremely long, set very low, and fall in graceful folds, the lower parts curling inwards and backwards.

Wrinkle: The head is furnished with an amount of loose skin which in nearly every position appears superabundant, but more particularly so when the head is carried low; the skin then falls into loose, pendulous ridges and folds, especially over the forehead and sides of the face.

Nostrils: The nostrils are large and open.

Lips, Flews and Dewlap: In front the lips fall squarely, making a right angle with the upper line of the foreface, while behind they form deep, hanging flews, and being continued into the pendant folds of loose skin about the neck, constitute the dewlap, which is very pronounced. These characteristics are found, though in a lesser degree, in the bitch.

Neck, Shoulders and Chest: The neck is long, the shoulders muscular and well sloped backward; the ribs are well sprung; and the chest well let down between the forelegs, forming a deep keel.

Legs and Feet: The forelegs are straight and large in bone, with elbows squarely set; the feet strong and well knuckled up; the thighs and second thighs (gaskins) are very muscular; the hocks well bent and let down and squarely set.

Back and Loin: The back and loins are strong, the latter deep and slightly arched.

Stern: The stern is long and tapering, and set on rather high, with a moderate amount of hair underneath.

Gait: The gait is elastic, swinging and free, the stern being carried high, but not too much curled over the back.

Colour: The colours are black and tan, red and tan, and tawny; the darker colours being sometimes interspersed with lighter or badger-coloured hair, and sometimes flecked with white. A small amount of white is permissible on chest, feet and tip of stern.

'Visualizing the Standard'

The following article entitled 'Visualizing the Standard' is taken from a series of articles first published in the *American Bloodhound Club Bulletin*.

In presenting a series of 'visualizations' of the bloodhound standard, I have chosen to begin at the 'end', with the all important rear assembly of the hound. Though the standard uses few words to describe what to look for in the ideal dog, these same terms are well defined in books on anatomy and movement. For a thorough description of the dog's anatomy, the classic book on the subject is by McDowell Lyon. The following passages are quoted from his book, *The Dog in Action*, to further illustrate and complement the fine drawings by Phyllis Natanek.

From the American Bloodhound Standard:

Legs and feet: The thighs and second thighs (gaskins) are very muscular; the hocks well bent and let down and squarely set.

Back and loin: The back and loins are strong, the latter deep and slightly arched. Stern.... The stern is long and tapering, and set on rather high, with a moderate amount of hair underneath.

Gait: The gait is elastic, swinging and free, the stern being carried high, but not too much curled over the back.

McDowell Lyon explains, 'The request for "hocks well let down"... is another means of asking for a long set of bones between stifle and hock as well as a short set from hock joint to ground....

Hocks well let down improve the leverage action as regards endurance ... according to the laws of leverage, getting the joint close to the ground will lessen the amount of power required to move weight but will not move it as far with the same given power.

The best position for examining the true angulation of the rear assembly is to pose the dog so that a perpendicular line dropped from the point of the buttock coincides with the front line of the bones below the hock joint.... In this position the pelvis should show its 30-degree angle with the bones below the hock joint standing vertical and the stifle taking whatever angle it possesses. If the pad is carried forward it will induce more bend in the stifle and may steepen the croup and also make the dog show sickle hocked.'

Regarding the loin ... 'The majority of standards ask for a slightly arched loin in an effort to gain the strength that a keystone gives an unsupported span in structural work. The arched loin is not to be confused with the camel or roach back, both of which are generally as undesirable as sway or soft back.'

The tail ... 'is a barometer to the set of the pelvis and the value of the muscles attached to the pelvis and croup.' Many old timers picked their dogs by the size of the tail at its base. (Indeed, at one benched show, an ancient lady strolled by and picked her favorites by looking at the base of the tail). 'A dog is no better than his tail' has been said often.

Two muscles activate the top side of the tail and one the bottom. If the tail is curled, 'sickle' or 'squirreled' continuously when this is not characteristic, it is not that the top muscles have become more tense but that the one on the bottom has lost or did not have sufficient tension.

Even as the dog begins with his head, he ends with his tail and by it many a story is told for it expresses health, mental attitude and what may be expected in the rest of the spinal column. Beware of any type tail that is not normally characteristic of the specific breed.

The following illustrations from this article help to show clearly what is meant by good proportion, posture and movement in the bloodhound.

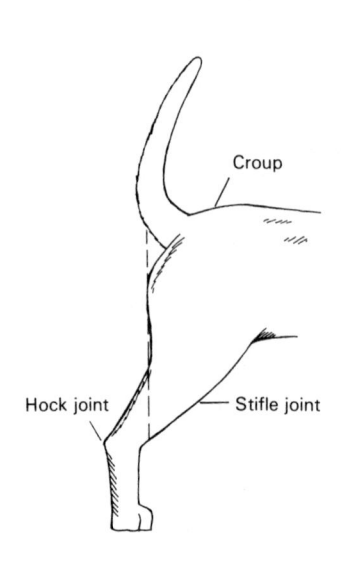

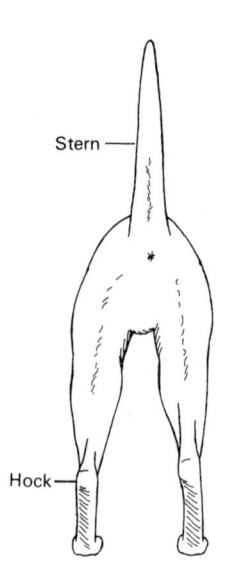

A good rear
'Scimitar' stern, well set on slight slope of croup. Good angulation at stifle and hock joints. Short, straight hock. Tight feet point straight ahead. Hound is well muscled in thigh and stands neither too wide nor too close.

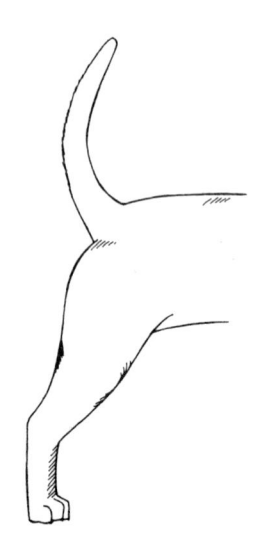

Cowhocked
Hocks incline inwards. Feet point out. Stifle inclines outwards.

88

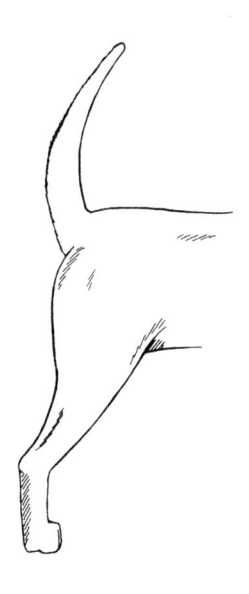

Straight stifled
Little or no angulation at stifle and hock joints.

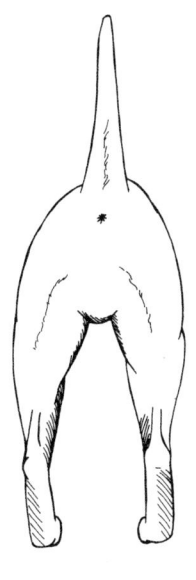

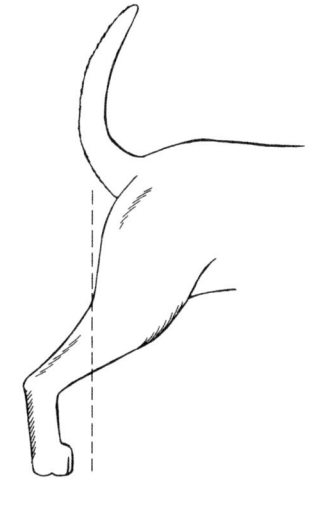

Bandy legged
Thigh bone and hock curve out. Feet point in.

Over-angulated
Front of hock should be up to dotted line.

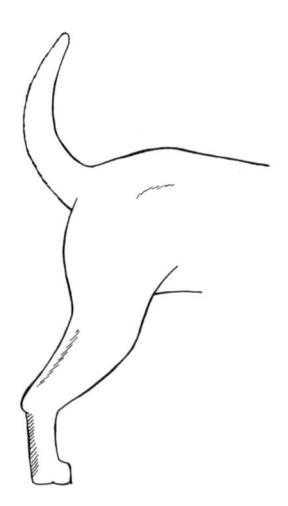

Goose rumped (steep in croup)
Croup 'falls away', causing also a
low tail set.

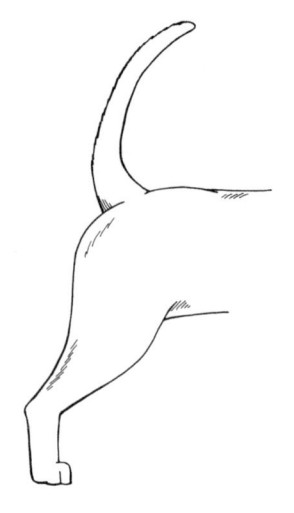

Flat in croup
Croup must not be totally flat, but
just *slightly* sloped.

Squirrel tail

Ring tail

Sickle hocks
Hound stands with hocks perpetually
bent, unable to straighten them.

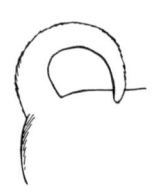

Wry tail

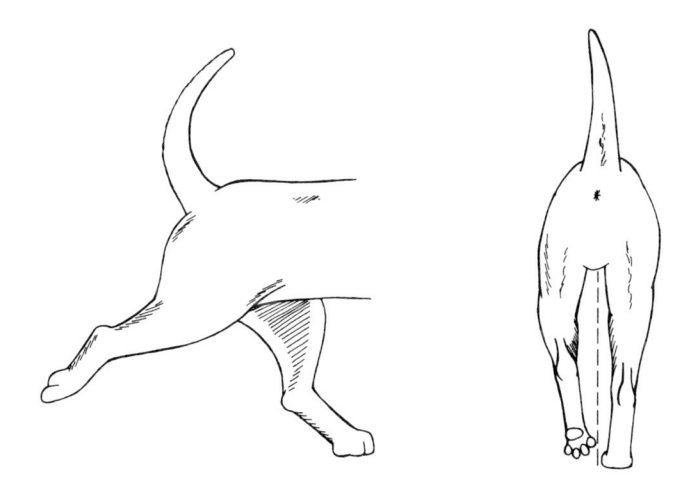

Good rear movement
Well carried stern. Good drive and follow through. Straight column of bone from hip to foot. As speed increases, feet tend towards centre of gravity (dotted line).

Sickle hocks
At a good, moderate trot, hock should 'follow through' and straighten as indicated by dotted line.

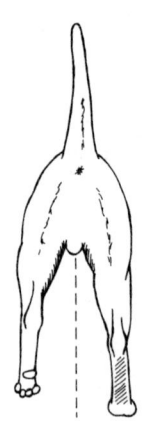

Moving wide
This dog makes no attempt to get his feet onto the centre of gravity (dotted line).

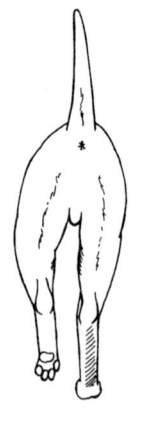

Moving close (also referred to as 'dusting a hock')
Straight line from hip to foot breaks at hock.

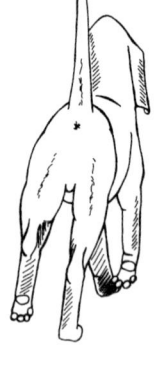

Crabbing (sidewinding)
Both rear legs move to one side of front legs, usually to avoid interference. The dog moves forward sideways.

Moving 'out of line' — cowhocked

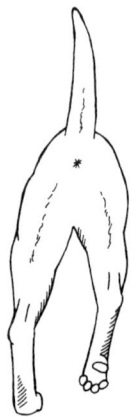

Moving 'out of line' — hocks bent outwards

Centre line of shoulder blade

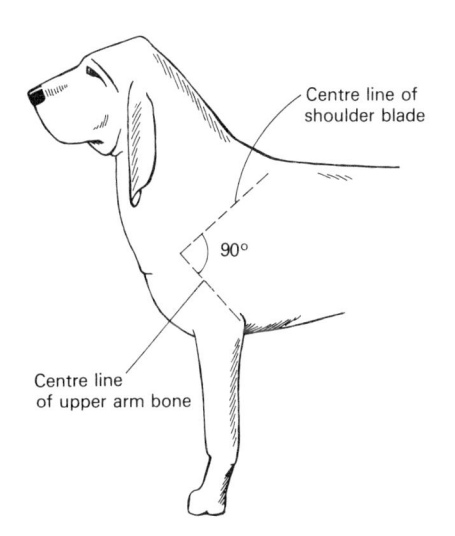

90°

Centre line of upper arm bone

A good front
Good length of neck. Shoulder blade sloped well back. Good forechest. Upper arm about same length as shoulder blade. Forelegs set well under body. Strong pastern with slight bend.

Straight shoulders
Point of shoulders (withers) in neck. Dip behind blade pronounced, usually with a roll of skin. Usually a lack of forechest. Forelegs set forward on body.

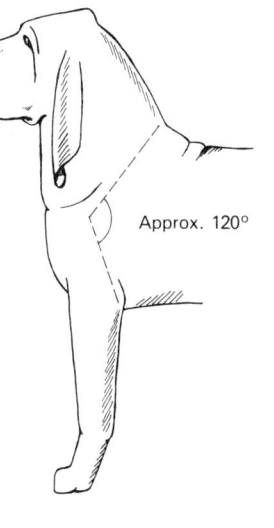

Approx. 120°

Short upper arm
Correct shoulder blade but the bone of the upper arm should be as long as the shoulder blade.
Legs set forward on body.

A good front
Elbows close to body. Shoulders muscled, but not loaded. Hound stands neither too wide or too narrow. Bones of forelegs strong and straight. Tight, well knuckled feet point almost straight ahead.

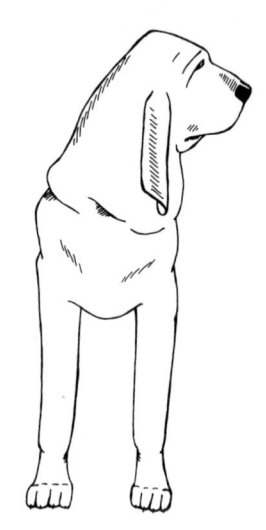

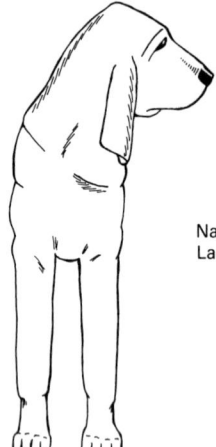

Narrow front
Lack of breadth in forechest.

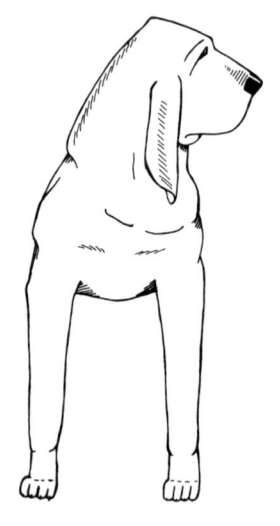

Wide loaded shoulders
Shoulders and elbows are pushed out from body. Usually seen on a hound with a weak rear who carries his weight on the forefeet.

Fiddle front (also called French front)
Elbows inclined outwards. Forearm bent. East-west feet.

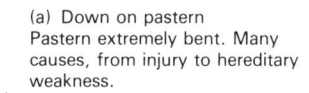

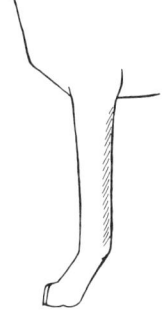

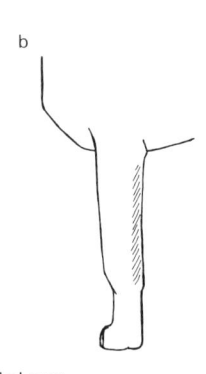

a

(a) Down on pastern
Pastern extremely bent. Many causes, from injury to hereditary weakness.

b

(b) Knuckled over
Pastern is stiff as a board. It will break down and often the foreleg quivers at a stand.

Pigeon toed
Forefeet point in.

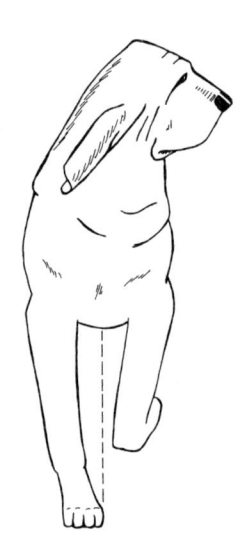

Good front movement — moderate trot
Forelegs straight from shoulder to foot. Feet converge toward centre of gravity (dotted line).

Very little bounce to the withers, indicating good shoulders. Good, straight extension of forelegs. Hound moves efficiently forward.

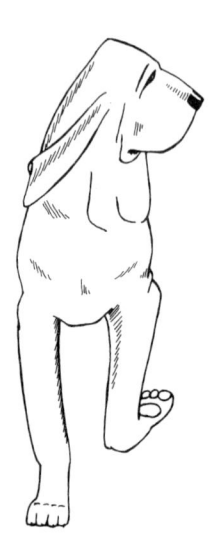

Paddling
This hound usually runs 'downhill', placing his weight on the forefeet. Hound throws feet out to side; awkward and inefficient.

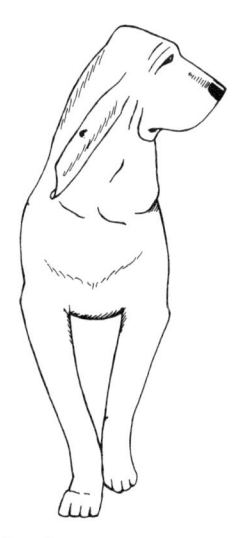

Moving close
Straight column of bone from
shoulder to foot breaks at pastern.

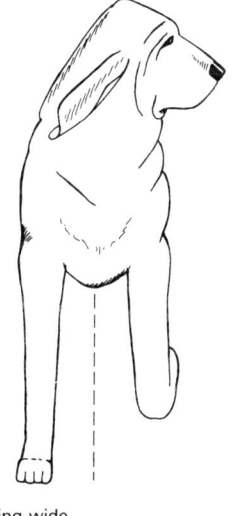

Moving wide
The hound makes no attempt to
place his feet near the centre of
gravity. This type of movement tires
the hound very quickly.

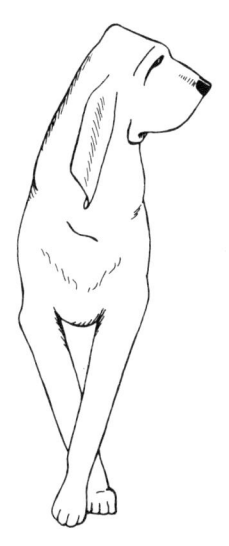

Crossing over
Very inefficient.

Toeing-in and out at elbows
Elbows out and feet turn in.

Hackney gait
Foreleg lifted high. Pastern bent. This action is usually the result of a good shoulder, but short upper arm. It is very flashy, but a total waste of motion for efficiency.

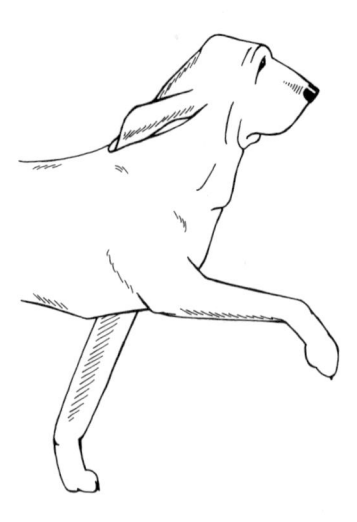

Over-reaching — padding
When the hound's foot comes down, the tension on the pastern will be excessive. Usually caused by slightly straight shoulders and an excellent rear drive.

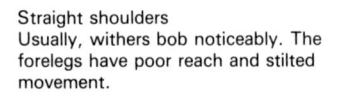

Straight shoulders
Usually, withers bob noticeably. The forelegs have poor reach and stilted movement.

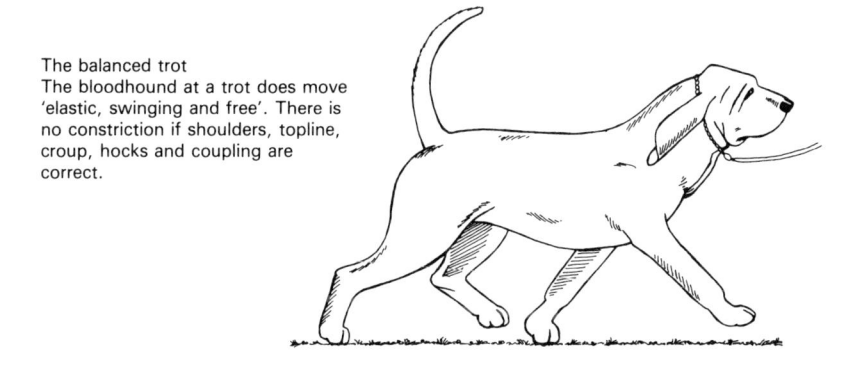

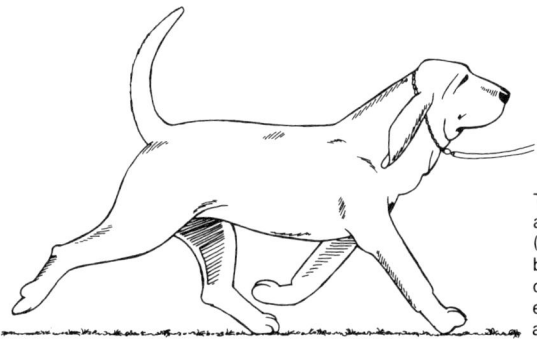

The balanced trot
The bloodhound at a trot does move 'elastic, swinging and free'. There is no constriction if shoulders, topline, croup, hocks and coupling are correct.

Topline stays level, reach and drive are matched, there is no crabbing (the forelegs move a split second before the rear), and the stern is well carried. The hound moves effortlessly, smoothly, appearing able to go on for ever.

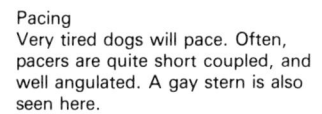

Pacing
Very tired dogs will pace. Often, pacers are quite short coupled, and well angulated. A gay stern is also seen here.

Dip in topline

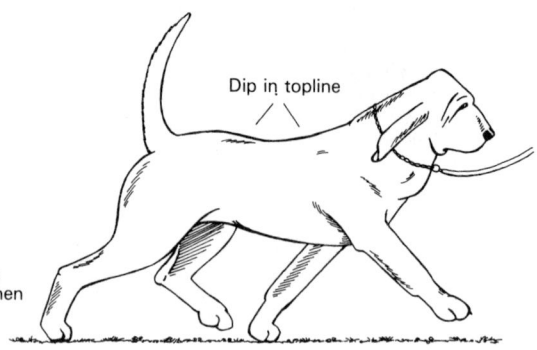

Soft back
Often, a hound that stands with a firm topline reveals a soft back when moving. This fault lessens endurance.

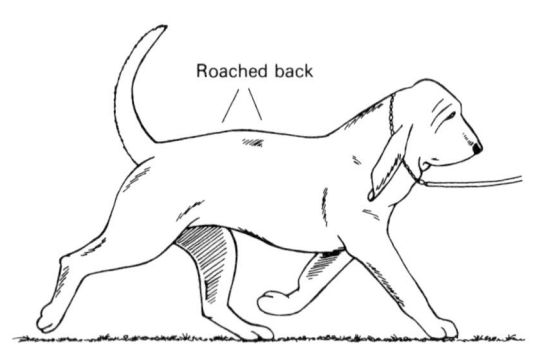

Roached back

Roach back
If a hound stands and moves with a permanent roach, something is put together wrong! Often, such a hound moves with his rear going every direction (rubber-legs).

Poor movement — stilted
Here is a hound with a straight front and straight rear. There is little reach or drive, and endurance will be poor afield.

100

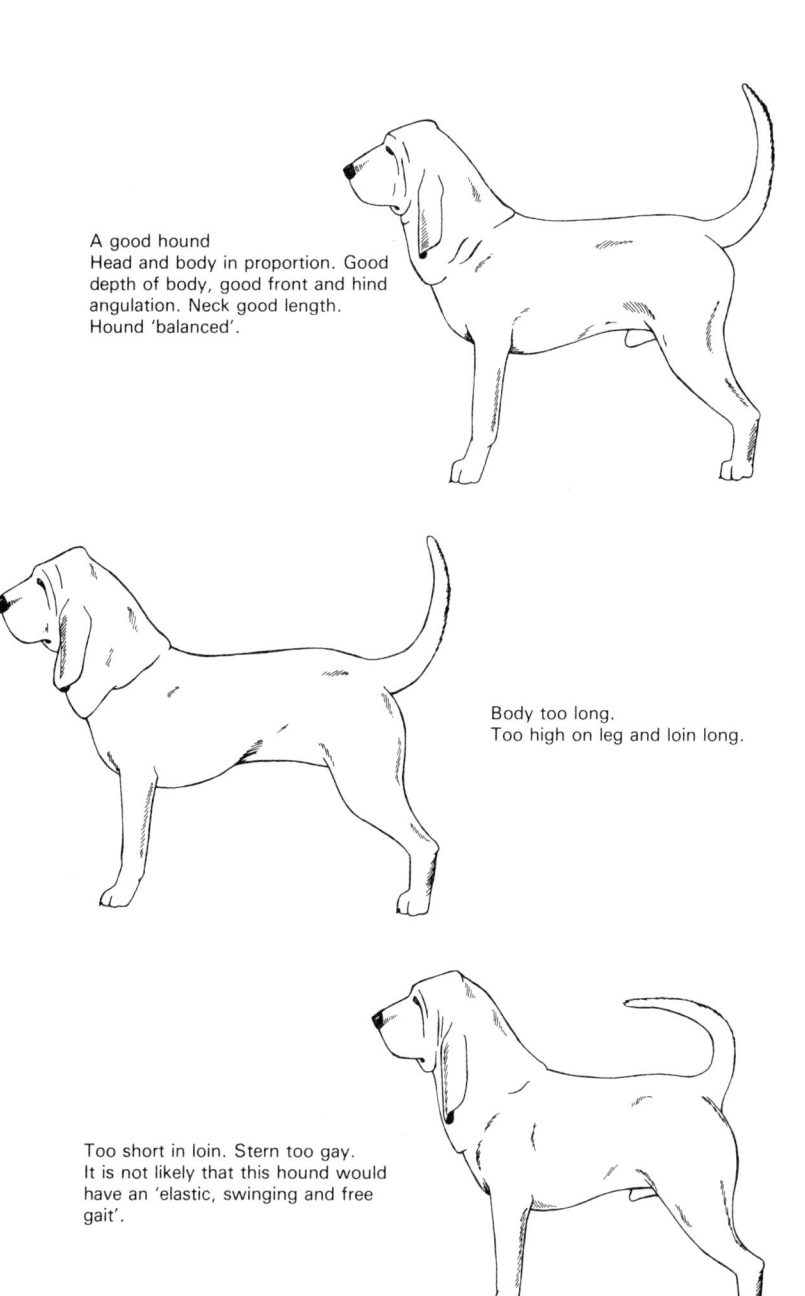

A good hound
Head and body in proportion. Good depth of body, good front and hind angulation. Neck good length. Hound 'balanced'.

Body too long.
Too high on leg and loin long.

Too short in loin. Stern too gay. It is not likely that this hound would have an 'elastic, swinging and free gait'.

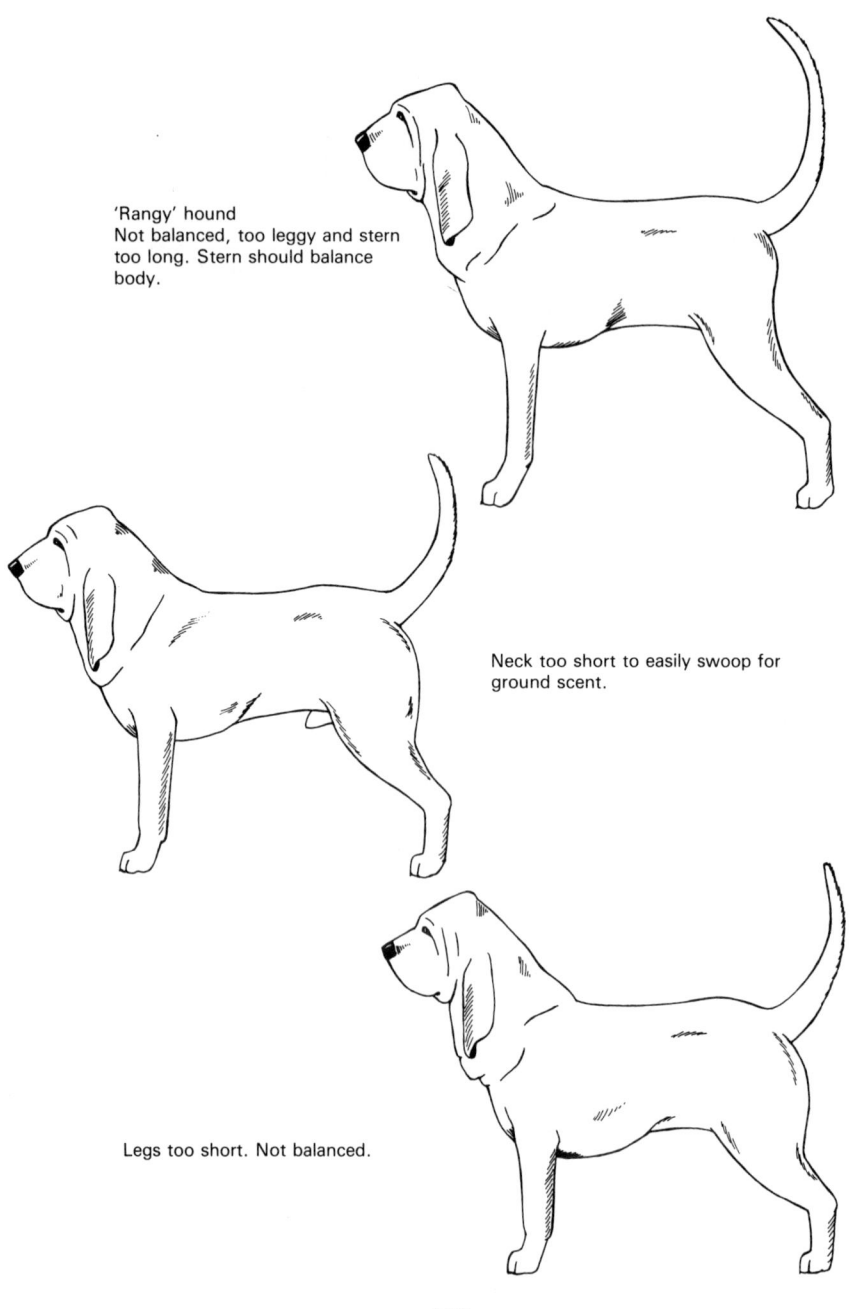

'Rangy' hound
Not balanced, too leggy and stern too long. Stern should balance body.

Neck too short to easily swoop for ground scent.

Legs too short. Not balanced.

'Ewe' neck, sway back and goose rump. Not enough 'lip'.

Topline arched. Incorrect whether standing or moving.

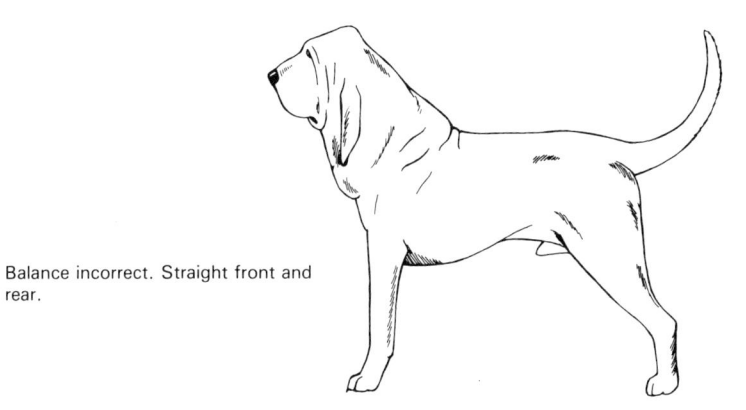

Balance incorrect. Straight front and rear.

It is more than likely that many will disagree with my views on showing and the Standard. However, it is not my intention to upset owners and breeders of this unique hound; I merely wish to promote the protection of the breed's natural qualities, and to ensure that the bloodhound remains a functional athlete for the purpose for which he was originally bred – that of work.

4
Working Trials

The sections on 'Organisation' and 'Judging at Trials' in this chapter have been contributed by Bobbie Edwards.

'Bloodhound working trials are held to promote the use of bloodhounds and the maintenance of a standard of proficiency in 'hunting the clean boot'. In Britain, the two bloodhound societies – the Association of Bloodhound Breeders and the Bloodhound Club – each hold two trials per year: one in the spring and one in the autumn. At the present time, these four events are the only trials organised in Britain, apart from some more senior events which are entered by invitation only.

Trials are regulated by the Kennel Club rules laid down for general breed working trials, as well as those set out specifically for bloodhounds (see Appendix 1), and must not be held without the prior permission of the Kennel Club. As specified in the rules, there are four stakes of differing standard (see Appendix 1) – Novice, Junior, Intermediate and Senior – in each trial, and various prizes, trophies and certificates to be won, the most coveted of which is the Kennel Club Tracking Certificate for Bloodhounds (or Working Trial Certificate). A hound becomes a Working Trial Champion (WTCh.) by winning Working Trial Certificates at two Senior Stakes under two different judges.

Apart from the overall objective of generally fostering an interest in the breed, the purpose of working trials is to test each bloodhound's ability to follow the scent trail of a man or, as it is more colourfully called, to 'hunt the clean boot'. This is done by judging the hound while it follows the scent trail of a runner along a predetermined route, known as a line. The difficulty of a line is varied by altering two factors: the length and the coldness (the length of time between the trail being laid and the hound starting). For instance, in the Novice Stake the lines are 1 mile (1·6 km) long, half an hour cold; in the Junior Stake they are 2 miles (3·2 km) long, one hour cold; in the Intermediate Stake they are 2½ miles (4 km) long, one and a half hours cold; and in the Senior Stake they are 3 miles (4·8 km) long, two hours cold.

Before a hound is allowed to compete in a working trial, it must obtain a Restricted Working Permit, by hunting a one-mile long line, half an hour cold under the observation of a qualified judge, and complete it within thirty minutes without any help. This first permit entitles the hound to hunt at trials on a leash. To hunt 'free' the hound must pass a further test which involves being hunted in stock. A judge must put the hound through farm stock, particu-

The author with his hound, Shylock of Stanwell, a good working hound noted for his fitness and voice.

larly sheep, both in hunting a line and simply walking, and be convinced that the hound can be trusted not to riot.

A Working Permit (restricted or full) is only valid for four consecutive trials, whether the hound is entered for them or not, unless the hound gains a Certificate of Merit or Working Certificate (or higher award) in that time. If the hound has not gained a Certificate by the time the permit expires, it must be retested before being allowed to enter another trial. This system prevents a poor hound from gaining a permit and then hunting at trials for years, never winning anything and just wasting its time.

A hound can only be entered in one stake at a trial (although it may be nominated for another), and if it wins that one, it must enter a higher stake next time. Hounds that have been successful in the Senior Stakes have the opportunity to compete for the Kelperland and Brough trophies, which are run separately from the trials and are entered by invitation only. These involve four, six and sometimes even twelve-hour cold lines.

Despite the rules and regulations, trials should not just be considered as competitions; they are also instructive – a great deal can be learnt from an experienced judge – and, of course, enjoyable social occasions. Competitors and spectators come from all over the country to hunt their hounds or to watch, enjoying a day in the fresh country air followed by a friendly get-together with fellow bloodhound owners and enthusiasts in the evening.

Organisation

This section describes in detail the organisation of a typical working trial in Britain. To write this, I have drawn from my direct experience with British trials, but there is no reason why it should not be adapted to conditions in almost any country in the world.

If the organisation of working trials is not carried out with enthusiasm, skill and imagination, much of the excitement to be gained from hunting with bloodhounds is lost for both hound and handler. Sloppy, thoughtless organisation leads to unfairness and delays for competitors and spectators.

It is hoped that this detailed description of the organisation of a working trial from beginning to end will act as a guide to promote interest in this most enjoyable sport.

Land

The first requirement when setting out to organise a working trial is suitable land. This is obtained from one or a combination of three sources: common land, large country estates, and small farmers. The first two are obviously the easiest to arrange, as there are fewer people to approach for the necessary permission – an amazing number of people can own the quantity of land required if it is broken up into small farms, and it is a very time-consuming business to go to all of them and explain exactly why you want to use it.

Permission should be obtained from all who have an interest in the land, including owners, tenant farmers, the local hunt, and those who have the shooting or grazing rights.

This part of the organisation must be carried out with great tact and care. Frequently, owner-farmers who are unfamiliar with the sport, imagine that it will involve hordes of horses and a ferocious pack of hounds trampling over their crops and rioting their livestock. If this impression is not corrected, it will obviously lead to many refusals. They must be convinced that their fears are unfounded and that it will really be a very quiet affair, the only possible problem being that of getting their tractors past the cars in the farm lanes. An approach to the local Master of Foxhounds for an introduction to the farmers in his country can prove invaluable.

It is impossible to give a hard and fast rule as to the quantity of land required for trials, as it is dependent upon the type of terrain, accessibility, the suitability of each field, the way it is broken up, etc. However, it is generally found that something in the region of 5000 acres (about 2000 hectares) is adequate. More land is needed where there are no natural boundaries, particularly in common land, because it is more difficult to read maps correctly and so the

A line should go through varied terrain!

runner is more likely to deviate from his route. The scent is also more likely to drift where there are no thick hedges and woods, particularly on very flat country.

There is a present tendency to use more land than is actually necessary, which does not help in organising trials efficiently. It is much better to use a small area, known thoroughly, than vast tracts of uncharted fields containing all kinds of unforeseen problems. There should, of course, be enough land for lines on each day to be laid on different ground, but it is not necessary to have separate land for each stake. The same land can be covered in alternative ways on subsequent days so that the competitors are still in the dark as to where their line goes. On one occasion recently, when there was a shortage of land, the same ground was even successfully used twice in the same day, with the lines going in varying directions. It is, however, important to ensure that consecutive lines do not cross or go too close to each other, and that no line doubles back so sharply that the hound, in making a wide sweeping cast, could pick it up farther on and miss out a section.

Licence Application

Having found suitable land and obtained permission to use it, and having chosen a date for the trials, the next step is to apply for a licence from the Kennel Club. Working trials may not be held in Britain without the prior permission of the Kennel Club and this must be applied for many months ahead of the proposed date. At the time of writing, applications are seldom refused. There are only two breed clubs involved and the only likely problem would be if a general breed working trial society were proposing to use the same land on the same date. It is, of course, natural courtesy to consult with the other bloodhound breed club when formulating your plans.

When the licence application form arrives from the Kennel Club, indicating that the proposed venue and date are acceptable, it must be signed by the Chairman, Treasurer and Secretary of the organising society and returned with the appropriate fee.

Judges

The next task is the appointment of the judges and as these must also be approved several months in advance by the Kennel Club, forward planning is essential. The initial selection of suitable candidates is usually made by a committee of the organising society, but it is important to guide them in this, and to ensure that they know what qualities to look for. The essential factor to consider in a judge is his knowledge of general hound work. This is far more important than fitness, age or any other consideration: it is always possible to arrange lines so that an older or slower judge can see from view points or by cutting corners.

There is a great deal to be learnt from an experienced hound man, and the working masters of the local hunts (not the society chaps who buy their way into a hunt, but those who have hunted all their lives) and huntsmen usually make ideal judges. Their knowledge of hounds and the country is easily adapted to the judging of the stakes, and they should be capable of giving a valuable opinion. If they have no previous experience of bloodhounds, it is best to explain the purpose of bloodhound work and how it differs from other hound work, so that they fully understand the objectives. If you tell them to imagine that they are searching for a lost child, and are choosing a hound to find it, they will immediately appreciate the qualities needed. It is also usually best to ask people new to bloodhound work to act as assistant judges in the first instance, before tackling a stake in their full capacity as judge.

Beware of appointing hunt followers on the strength of their hunting experience; the 'field' rarely gets a proper chance to see real hound work, and merely hunting regularly is no qualification for an adequate judge. Judges coming up from the ranks of the handlers should have had plenty of experience in handling hounds successfully in all the stakes, and should have been active participants at trials as stewards, assistant judges, runners, etc. for many years.

When asking people to judge, it is wise to use the telephone initially and write to confirm the appointment when you have their affirmation; you can waste a great deal of precious time waiting for an answer to a letter of invitation. You should also determine at this stage whether they wish to judge on foot or on horseback: they may need to be provided with a suitable horse or stabling for their own horse.

Once the judges have accepted their appointments (preferably in writing), their names must be sent to the Kennel Club for approval. If this is the first time, the proposed judge must fill in a questionnaire to be forwarded to the Kennel Club. For a Senior Stake, the Club will not approve a judge who has not officiated before, and their decision on the approval of all Championship Trial judges is final, so it is as well to make sure that the selection is good in the first place or embarrassment will be caused and much time will have been wasted.

The Kennel Club committee which approves judges, meets at infrequent intervals, so this part of the organisation must take place well in advance. It is not necessary for judges to be approved at other than Championship Trials, but as the breed societies only hold Championship Trials and the more senior Member's Stakes, where only the most respected judges are appointed, this means in practice, all judges.

Schedules

When the chosen judges have been approved, two draft schedules should be prepared giving all the details of the trials, the time of the draw and the closing date for entries. These must be sent to and approved by the Kennel Club before the licence will be issued. The schedules should also draw attention to the special rules and conditions that apply to bloodhound trials, as well as the general rules and regulations governing all working trials (with a few exceptions). The entry forms are also included with the schedules.

The final schedule should be prepared and copies sent to the Kennel Club and all likely competitors as soon as the licence has been issued. Some should also be kept in reserve for unexpected enquirers.

Assistant Judges

Two assistant judges for each stake should also be appointed. Although these do not have the same authority as the judge, care should still be observed in their choice. Sometimes the committee of the organising society selects them, but often they are left to the working trial secretary.

It is particularly important that the assistant judges chosen for the later, more senior stakes be well versed and experienced in bloodhound work, so that, should the judge have to leave a hound, or for any other reason have to ask the assistant's opinion, he can be relied upon to give a competent assessment.

If there are a large number of hounds in a stake or the hunting is slow because of poor scenting conditions, hounds are frequently started long before the preceding one has finished its line. This makes it physically impossible for the judge himself to watch the complete line for every hound. In these cases, it has been found valuable for the two assistants to take alternate hounds from beginning to end, so that at the end of the day, each assistant has seen all the work of half the hounds, and can tell the judge how the work continued after he had to leave.

Surveying

The next step is to begin to survey the land. This is perhaps the most important part of the organiser's job, and, if it is carried out conscientiously in the early stages, it makes the whole task much easier.

An enormous amount of time can be saved initially by studying the estate's own maps, where possible. These frequently show the type of crops in each field and sometimes the means of access to the field. They are usually quite up to date and show recent alterations.

When going round the farms to ask permission it is a good idea to arm yourself with a large scale map (ideally one which shows contours and fields, e.g. 1:25,000) so that you can mark in any boundaries or information about the land which the farmer tells you. Boundaries are particularly important because it is usually fairly easy to get from one field to another on a farm, but quite another matter to cross a boundary from one farm to another. Farmers will often be very helpful, showing where hedges have been removed, land drained, woods cleared, etc., all of which can be marked on the map.

After this, it is a case of going round the area in a car and getting to know it well. A great deal of work can be done from view points, using a pair of binoculars, and any information should be marked on the map as it is discovered.

Important information includes: crops in each field and their likely state of growth at the time of the trials; altered hedges and fences; removed woods and new plantations; position of and condition of gates; gaps in hedges and fences; impossibly deep or wide streams or rivers; excessively thick hedges, undergrowth or forests; railway lines, fast roads or other hazards; occupied houses, building work, forestry work, scout camps or other signs of human activity; access roads and tracks, making a note of their state, if wet, and turning points and widths; stock – not forgetting that if surveying in winter, by the time the spring trials are held, the cattle may have been put out into the fields, and what was an empty piece of pasture when you saw it, may have three hundred head of cattle on it when the unfortunate hound and handler face it.

As well as the 1:25,000 map, you should also have a larger scale map (preferably 1:10,000) of the area mounted on a board. At the end of the day, the information gleaned during the survey can be transferred to this map. Features which have been removed subsequent to the map being made, can be whited out with correcting fluid and new items inserted in thin, black ball point pen. A colour code for fields can be used to great advantage, for instance, pale green indicating grazing, brown for plough, dark green for woods, red for forbidden areas, etc., as this will help considerably when planning lines.

The reasons for using the two sizes of map are that although the large 1:10,000 map is good for planning and showing judges and runners the details of the lines, the 1:25,000 is much easier to carry in the trials. It also shows a large surrounding area which helps to orientate judges or runners with distant landmarks, it shows contours and is easily folded to pocket size while still showing enough to be useful, particularly when riding.

When the use of binoculars from roads has yielded all the secrets it can, there is nothing for it but to start using one's feet and walk around until all the fields have been checked.

Whilst walking and driving around the area, it is a good policy to note land which will not be visible to spectators. You can then plan the lines avoiding these areas, giving the followers maximum opportunity to watch the hounds at work. It is very boring for spectators if lines are laid in such a way that they can only be seen at the beginning and end. Some country, of course, does not lend itself to spectators, but every effort should be made to make the trials as interesting as possible, to foster enthusiasm for the sport.

In country with good visibility, colour photographs can be of tremendous help both for planning lines and for showing runners and judges the lines. An instant camera is useful for this.

Planning the Lines

Having surveyed the whole area and walked through as much of it as possible, you are now ready to start marking in the lines. This should be done as early as possible, although it is often left until only a week or two before the trials, and sometimes is even done the night before. This does not show good organisation and it is certainly very unsatisfactory to plan the lines each day for the following stake; after a long, hard day it is difficult to give the matter sufficient thought to make the lines good.

As soon as the date for the close of entries has passed, you will know the number of hounds entered and can therefore start on the lines. It is just as well to plan an extra line or two for each stake, in case a re-run is needed for some reason. It is also necessary to be fairly flexible in your plans to allow for unforeseen problems such as unexpected farm activity which may need to be avoided.

First of all, mount the large scale, coloured-in map on a board and cover it with thick transparent plastic. Arm yourself with a tape measure, thread or fuse wire, a chinagraph pencil, and, of course, the photographs and other information collected. It is a good idea to work on site, if possible, whilst planning the lines for each stake.

Study the map carefully, and decide on a general plan of action: starting the first line as near as possible to the meet, aiming to stop at lunchtime in a suitable spot, perhaps by a pub which serves snacks or a barn for shelter in case the weather is bad, and finishing at the end of the day near a suitable place for the prizegiving.

There are three major factors to be taken into consideration when planning lines: fairness to the hounds and handlers, requirements of the judges and enjoyment for the spectators.

The most important of these is, of course, fairness. All too often one hound is seen cantering round a line in lush new wheat or meadow and another struggles with a line consisting entirely of bare plough. This situation obviously makes it very difficult for the judge to assess comparative merit and leads to criticism from the competitors. Most competitors accept set-backs with a sporting spirit, but it is frustrating to be told that it is the 'luck of the draw' when one line is in totally different terrain from another. If the organiser does his homework properly, surveying thoroughly and thinking carefully, this situation should not arise. The 'luck of the draw' should only cover factors beyond the organiser's control, such as sudden changes in the weather, unexpected farm work, hikers, etc.

This is not to say that lines should not incorporate difficulties for the hound. Each line should give a variety of ground conditions, sharp turns, fences and gates so that the judge can assess the hound's ability to cope with problems.

It is worth mentioning here that I personally feel that the deliberate road crossing frequently made on more difficult stakes is a complete waste of time and a very dangerous practice. The width of a road is not sufficient to deter the hound from picking up the scent on the far side with a very small cast, and all experienced handlers know that the crossing is usually clearly marked by a gap between the parked cars of the convoy. It is far better to plot the line along a farm track for a hundred paces or so, to test the hound's performance on a hard surface and in picking up the exit point.

It is very important to give each hound a start on good scenting ground to get his nose properly accustomed to the body scent of the person he is expected to follow. A hound with a good start will be able to cope with a bad scenting patch further on, but if the start is bad he may never get going at all.

Consideration must next be given to your judges. A mounted judge will require lines quite different from those for a foot judge. There are advantages in both horse and foot as a means of transport for judges, but both set different problems which must be understood.

With a horse, distance is of lesser importance, but access is vital and lines should be laid so that they can be easily followed, bearing in mind that few judges are adept jumpers, particularly on borrowed horses, which are often inadequate for the task in any case. A mounted judge has, however, the considerable advantage of height, and does not need to follow the hounds quite so closely as a foot judge, as he need not fear being left behind. Bearing these points in mind, the line should be laid reasonably close to, but not necessarily through gaps and gates, whilst avoiding wire fencing, and bogs which will not carry the horse's weight.

The judge's map should show not only the route he must take to follow within reasonable distance, but also getaway routes should he have to leave a slow hound to start the next line, so that he can avoid having to ride up the first hound's line to get to the next. In a big stake of course, distance can also be a problem and it may be necessary to arrange for a change of horses at lunchtime. It is vital that the horses should not have to hack more than is absolutely essential.

With foot judges the problems are quite different. Unless he is very young and active, it is necessary to save the judge's legs as much as possible. This can be done by making the lines twisty, by using viewpoints to full advantage and by making sure that the getaway route leads quickly to the start of the next line. Arrangements can be made to pick up the judge on a convenient road part way along the line. Distances to and from meeting places and between lines are not so important where foot judges are officiating as they can be transported by car.

The final major consideration to be made is to the spectators. Ideally, the lines should be arranged with as little turning and movement of the convoy of observers as possible. It is very time-consuming to have to drive miles around the countryside from one start to the next, especially bearing in mind that someone (probably you) will have to take runners forward to walk their lines and later get back to the convoy in order to start the next competitor and pick up another runner for the next line. There have been trials in which the lines jumped backwards and forwards between two roads; a mile for the hounds, but seven or more for the convoy. Turning twenty cars in a narrow lane is no joke. It is much better if the lines can be arranged to follow a natural pattern forward along a road, working on each side of it, and, if necessary, returning to fill in the gaps between the lines already arranged.

If there are view points, use them. Lines are far more interesting if long stretches can be seen from one spot.

Apart from these three major considerations, there are several points worth remembering.

Starts and finishes should be as close to a road as possible; a long walk to a start can cause a delay which should be avoided.

A few deliberate turns are generally a good policy, particularly in country where the scenting conditions are fairly constant, such as moorland, or where there are no boundaries such as hedges where the direction might naturally change. Remember too, that the wind has a strong effect on scenting and since you will not know the wind direction until the day of the trials, it is best to introduce several turns to counteract any unfair advantages and to give a variety of problems.

Scent can also drift a considerable distance on a windy day. If you are short of land, it is better for a line to cross a subsequent (but not consecutive) line than for it to double back too close to itself. Consecutive lines should be separated by some distance or, better still, laid on opposite sides of the road you are working from, so that if a hound goes wrong it does not have to be called off for fear of fouling the next line.

Bearing all the above points in mind, roughly sketch in the lines for one stake on a large map, using a chinagraph pencil. Then go back and measure each line accurately and mark it in properly, using the piece of thread or wire to check the distances with great care. When you are satisfied that they are correct, mark them all in on the small scale map.

Having plotted all the lines for one stake, not forgetting an extra one or two in case a line has to be re-run, do the same for the other stakes. Try to make them as varied as possible; it is bad planning simply to join two Novice Stake lines to make one Junior Stake line etc., as competitors frequently watch the whole trials and they should obviously have no prior knowledge of the direction of their line. Also avoid repeating any patterns; wily handlers, watching hounds working on the previous days, can guess the direction of the line and save time by knowledgeable casts. Sometimes, of course, it is inevitable that a particular bridge or gate must be used, but it can usually be approached and left in various ways. Even reversing the order of the lines can confuse handlers, but it must be remembered that, even if they are aware of the general direction of a line, their hounds must hunt accurately if they are to convince a knowledgeable judge.

Finally, check the lines by going back to the area and looking them over on the spot, making sure that no silly mistakes have been made.

Maps

Maps must now be prepared for the judges, assistant judges, stewards, runners and organisers.

Each judge and assistant judge will need a map showing all the lines for his stake. The routes and getaway routes for a mounted judge should be marked in separate colours and the pick up points for foot judges should be clearly shown.

For each runner you must mark a separate map showing just the one line to be walked. It is particularly important that this is done accurately and is *exactly* the same as the route shown on the judge's map. If the runner makes a mistake and goes the wrong way, he should correct this map and show it to the judge before the hound is laid on. Write the time at which the line is scheduled to be walked and any specific problems of which the runner should be aware, on the back.

On all the maps, each line should be marked S for Start and F for Finish and numbered at each end.

You will also need a waterproofed map showing the route the convoy of spectators is to take, but not the lines, which can be pinned up at the meet to show latecomers where to find the convoy throughout the day.

The maps prepared for each stake should be put into a large folder together with any useful information gathered during surveying. Should the organiser be unable to attend the trials for some reason at the last minute, these folders should contain all the information and materials required, so that a substitute can take over with no difficulty.

It is a good idea to put all the maps in thin plastic bags to protect them and have extra marked maps for judges in reserve. The large scale coloured-in map will be very useful on the day for showing runners and judges the terrain in detail. This should not, of course, be marked with the lines until after each hound has set out.

Catalogues

When all the entries have been received, a proper draw must be made to decide the order of running of the hounds in each stake. After deciding the amount of time that can be allowed for each line on each day, a catalogue must be prepared, giving the details of the hounds as shown on the entry forms, the order of hunting, times of the lines and all other information that the competitors will need, not forgetting their telephone numbers in case they wish to exchange lines.

It is my opinion that in the Senior Stakes a minimum of one and a half hours should be allowed between lines, even if this means that some lines have to be carried over to the next day. All too often, the length of time is shortened simply because the judge cannot spare the number of days needed to do the job. If this is the case, the wrong judge has been chosen. Shortening the period between lines shortens the amount of time the judge can stay with one hound before going on to the next, and this often means that the judge does not have sufficient time to assess each hound's performance adequately.

Enough catalogues should be printed to supply all the competitors plus the judges, officials, spectators and landowners as well as leaving a few in reserve, as marked catalogues must be sent a few days after the trials to the Kennel Club, the dog papers, the secretary of the officiating society, and, as a courtesy, to the other breed society's secretary. It is helpful to the competitors to send them catalogues as early as possible so that they can make their own plans.

Local Arrangements

There are numerous local arrangements which should be made as early as possible, preferably whilst surveying the land, and which must be organised with care if the trials are to run smoothly.

Prizegiving Venue
The prizegiving and summing up is usually held in a public house at the end of each day, and most publicans welcome the extra custom early in the evening providing that they have been warned in advance and can arrange the necessary staff. When you can estimate the time of finishing each day, tell the publican when to expect the crowd, and, if it is a short day, enquire whether they can come in early before opening time, perhaps for tea. If a private room can be arranged, so much the better.

Horses for the Judges
Organising these can be a major problem and should not be dismissed too lightly. Carrying a judge for a full day is very exhausting for an unfit horse, so do try to get the best mounts available. Sometimes, if you are on good terms with the local hunt staff, it is possible to borrow a hunt horse, especially if the judge is a huntsman or Master of Foxhounds himself. Otherwise you may have to rely on the local riding school, which is not always very satisfactory. Check on the weight of the judge, his competence to ride and his preferences. Usually the best type of horse is one which is strong, quiet enough to stand still while the judge consults the map, makes notes and observes the hounds at work, but lively enough to canter on when required, and it is important that it is suited to the judge's weight.

Accommodation
If the judge has to travel any distance to get to the trials, it is usual to arrange his accommodation, either in an hotel or at a member's house. It is also appreciated if a local hotel and caravan site can be recommended in the schedule for the competitors. If the pub where the summing up is to take place provides accommodation, so much the better. All this helps to make the trials into an enjoyable social occasion.

More Appointments

Road Marshall
A road marshall should be appointed for each stake. His duties are to keep the convoy together, to keep the spectators informed and

the next competitor ready to work. He should ensure that roads are kept clear for other users and that gates are left closed. If lines cross roads, he should arrange for the traffic to be stopped whilst the hound is crossing and he must ensure that all hounds are kept under control and exercised in approved areas. He will need a properly marked map so that he can get the convoy to the correct places at the correct times, and so that after each hound has begun, he can show spectators which direction the hound should go and where the view points are. He should also make sure that the runner is in position at the end of the line ready to be identified and that, where applicable, there is a group of people at the end of a line.

Stake Manager
I am assuming that the organiser will be in overall charge of each stake throughout the trials. However, if he is an active participant at trials as a competitor, with so few chances to compete throughout the year, it would be unfair to expect him to stand down simply to benefit others. A separate manager, whose name should be announced in the schedule, can then be appointed for each stake that the organiser has entered. Ideally, he should be in charge of everything in that stake, from the marking up of the lines, through the day to the judge's summing up. However, it is not always possible for him to become thoroughly familiar with the land, and in these cases the overall organiser should map out all the lines in the usual way, giving plenty of space for his own line so that it may be altered by the stake manager. This is not as satisfactory as if the overall organiser has nothing to do with the planning of the stake in question, but is acceptable if the other competitors are aware of the situation. Problems arise, of course, if there are absentees, as the organiser can only hunt the unknown line and so cannot move forward in the catalogue in the usual way.

Judge's Stewards
Frequently judge's stewards are appointed. These are often local hunt followers who may enjoy a morning or afternoon watching hound work. They usually bring their own horses and prove

invaluable in their knowledge of the country. Comparative newcomers to the bloodhound scene can also be used for this purpose and they will find it very instructive. Usually there is no shortage of volunteers, but it is important that the distinction between them and assistant judges is made clear, and that their opinion of the hounds' work is not considered for the awarding of prizes.

Runners

Finally, runners must be organised. There are usually a number of volunteers in the bloodhound ranks who can be relied upon, but it is as well to make sure of a few, especially for the morning of the first day. You can also make use of local people but make sure that they can read a map accurately and have been briefed in the correct procedure to take when walking a line. The whole trials stands or falls on the accuracy and dependability of the runners, so it is vital that they can be trusted.

There is some controversy amongst bloodhound followers as to whether or not competitors should be used as runners.

I would prefer an experienced, reliable fellow competitor to walk a line for me than an unproved or unreliable volunteer, although obviously it is better to use someone who is not involved in that particular stake. They must of course be armed with suitable footwear and a smeller.

Final Arrangements

The judges, especially those officiating for the first time, and assistant judges should be sent a leaflet showing their duties, and giving advice on bloodhound trials, prizes to be awarded etc.

Prize cards and prize money should be on hand at the summing up after each stake and the holders of the trophies should therefore be reminded to return them in time. Flags must be made for the starts of each line and to mark road crossings or finishes where necessary. Plenty of flags should be supplied in reserve as it is surprising how many of them go missing.

It is usual to provide refreshment for judges during the day and at lunch times. A thermos of coffee or tea is always very welcome and a packed lunch or snack in a pub can be arranged at midday.

The judge should have a proper break at midday so that he can rest and recap on the morning's work before tackling the afternoon lines.

The Trials

At last the big day arrives and all your plans are complete. The essence of good organisation is to plan your campaign like a military exercise and to keep to a rigid timetable. Synchronise the officials', judges' and runners' watches at the meet. It is only too easy to lose ten minutes here and there, and, not only can this run into hours by the end of the day, but, more importantly, it will result in hounds getting lines hotter or colder than is correct for the stake. For instance, if you forget to put down a runner in good time, you will have to wait for the correct time lapse before the line can be hunted. Remember to allow enough time to get runners, judges and competitors to their starts. Make sure that the second competitor of the day is aware that if the first fails to turn up, he will be expected to hunt the first line instead.

You will have briefed your judge before the day as to his duties; however, it is a good idea to explain each line to him briefly just before the hound starts, in case there is any confusion with the map. He should also be told the time at which the next hound is scheduled to start, so that he can be sure to leave in good time to start it promptly. It is also sensible to remind him at this stage to avoid giving unintentional help to the handler by hanging back when the hound goes in the wrong direction or by cutting corners before the hound has shown clearly the direction of the line.

The assistant judges should also be briefed, particularly with regard to their instructions should the hound be slow, when it is usual for one assistant to continue with it, while the other goes on with the judge to the next line. The assistants should take notes during the day, in case the judge wishes to consult them at the end of the stake.

If there are any absentees, the hounds should be moved up in catalogue order to fill the spaces. If these are known in advance and it is a particularly crowded stake, it is possible to spread the lines out throughout the day so that the judge has more time to spend with each hound, but the competitors should be informed at the beginning of the day of any alterations. If any competitor is absent as the time approaches for his line, the following competitor should be ready to hunt the line. The first hound can be given the second line if it arrives within the half hour allowed, but if any later than that it should be disqualified.

It is most important to consider your runners. First of all, they must be given their maps well ahead of time so that they can study them and raise any queries. They should also be armed with two flags with which to mark the start, another to put on the road if his start is hidden and one more if he had to cross a road.

Each runner should be taken to the start in plenty of time so that landmarks can be pointed out, and arrangements should be made for him to be collected at the end of the line. It is very thoughtless to leave runners sitting around for hours, and if you do not look after them you will soon find yourself short of volunteers.

If the runner has a car, lead him to the end of his line first and leave his car there. Then drive him back to the start, pointing out landmarks as you go. This is particularly advantageous on the more senior stakes when he may have to wait for two to three hours between finishing the line and being identified by the hound. Having his own car at the end of the line will mean that he is quite independent, although he must remember to return his corrected map to the judge.

On colder lines, runners should mark the finishes so that they can stand on the exact spot later for identification. They should also leave and return to the finish in the same direction, where possible over a wall or other barrier which will check the hound.

At the end of the stake, the competitors, officials and spectators will all go to the place appointed for the judge's summing up, where they can relax with refreshments while waiting for the judge's decision.

Usually the stake manager withdraws with the judge so that he can remind him of the prizes and trophies to be awarded. He should also remind the Senior Stake judge of the Kennel Club rule regarding the awarding of the coveted Working Trial Certificate.

This must not be awarded unless sufficient merit has been shown by the best hound of the stake.

The stake manager should be available to answer questions on specific rules, but he must make no attempt to comment on any hound's work or try to influence the judge's decisions in any way.

When the judge has decided on the placings, the stake manager can complete the prize cards ready for the judge's signature. The most instructive and valuable part of the day arrives as the judge announces his decisions and gives his summing up. This should never be rushed as a great deal of hound advice can be gained from an experienced judge who is encouraged to impart it.

After the summing up, it is usual for the stake manager to thank all concerned for their help – as briefly as possible – and then the assembled gathering can unwind and discuss the day. This is the ideal moment for people to pick the judge's brains on hound work, and bloodhound work in particular.

Judging at Trials

Some years ago, I was asked to co-judge a Junior Stake with a young, but very knowledgeable huntsman. He arrived early at the meet, unboxed his horse and said, 'I've never seen a bloodhound work, what am I supposed to do?' I replied, 'Imagine there is a lost child on these moors, which hound would you choose to find him?' He thought a moment, then said, 'That's easy', and off we went.

We had a marvellous day, I learnt a great deal about hound work from him and by the evening we had individually come to the same conclusions. The hound that won was not particularly fast but was so certain of herself and so accurate that we knew that if her runner had fallen into a coomb, she would have been sure to have found him. The next two hounds placed were good, faster than our winner, but out-ran their handlers and lost confidence in their own ability when they found themselves alone. The others were unable to complete their lines without help, changed onto crossed lines or rioted on deer. My co-judge, because of his years of knowledge of general hound work, was able to read the bloodhounds better than I could, and in most cases better than their handlers. With the idea in mind that we were trying to find a lost child, he had no difficulty in picking out his prize winners.

It is interesting to note that nowadays, bloodhound working enthusiasts do not seem exactly sure what they are trying to achieve. Is this a sort of mini foxhunt using one hound and a human quarry? Or is this a simulated police tracking job? If the former, it is all very jolly and a good gallop would be the order of the day. If the latter, a steady progress at walking pace would be ideal. Because the bloodhound is so seldom used by the police in Britain, our trials are now more of a sport than a real test of bloodhound ability. If private owners were called out more for real work the emphasis would probably change, as it would if our judges came more from the ranks of the police and army instructors. As it is, our judges are very varied: hunt followers who owe their position more to their ability to ride to hounds than to their knowledge of hounds, working masters and huntsmen, and handlers who have gained sufficient experience through handling and assisting at trials. The best of these are those masters and

Bobbie Edwards and Ch. Sanguine Saint at the start of their Intermediate line, Autumn Bloodhound Club trials, 1979.

huntsmen who have worked with hounds all their lives and who appreciate the difference between the purpose of the bloodhound and that of their own pack.

I feel that competition work should be an attempt to assess a bloodhound's ability to hunt, sticking to his quarry's scent through thick and thin, and getting his man in the end through sheer persistence.

A good hound should display drive and keenness to work, concentration, ability to stick to the correct scent, good casting when the scent deteriorates, boldness, disregard for farm stock, game and crossed scents, agility in negotiating obstacles, and should be a pleasure to watch. Faults include changing to another scent, rioting on farm stock or wildlife, lack of enthusiasm and concentration, inability to negotiate obstacles, nervousness with quiet farm stock and farm vehicles, and being out of control of the handler.

In a real situation, the most important thing is to stick to the quarry's scent disregarding any other crossed line or distraction. Should the scent peter out for any reason, a reliable hound will at least have pointed the way and narrowed down the area to be searched, but if a hound cannot be trusted to keep to the proper scent he is not worth using. If he changes to another line, he is worse than useless, as he will actually be taking the searchers in the wrong direction. The trials judge should therefore take the finding of the runner by hound and handler without his assistance to be of first importance.

No Change or Riot

The good hound shows no tendency to change or riot. Even in the Novice Stake, freedom from change should be the first and most important criterion, and hounds should not be considered for any prizes if they have been guilty of changing. A problem arising at trials is that runners are not always reliable. Frequently judges trust their marked maps implicitly, forgetting that the runner is capable of misreading his map or the maps have possibly not been marked accurately, and the runner has not actually walked where the map says he should have done. Common sense should prevail too. It is unlikely that anyone other than the runner will have walked on a sticky ploughed field on a very wet day, and a hound taking the wrong route in these circumstances could be presumed to be correct if he continues to work methodically. On the other hand, if he suddenly rushes off along a path when he has been working slowly, it is likely that he has changed. By watching the hound's behaviour closely, a change should be instantly apparent.

Those judges who trust the map rather than the hound sometimes stop the hound, believing him to be guilty of this fault. This of course is very wrong – a hound who appears to be hunting well without any apparent alteration of speed or behaviour should always be left to get on with it without interference from the judge, who should always check with the runner as to the correct route at the finish. Even then I am more inclined to trust the hound than the runner; some are really not at all sure where they have been although they are loathe to admit it! Only careful questioning will elicit the truth, and asking for a description of landmarks *en route* can be very helpful.

A hound must, of course, disregard farm stock. A hound seen chasing sheep should be instantly disqualified and the working trial organiser informed. A hound should also be confident with quiet farm stock, although some young cattle and horses can be difficult and the judge can sometimes help to keep them back so that the hound can work out his line without being trampled or unduly frightened.

Drive

The next most important factor to consider in a bloodhound is drive, or the enthusiasm to work. This is particularly important to look for in a young hound; bad faults such as a tendency to change can be trained out, but a young hound showing a lack of drive will never improve. In fact, as hounds get older they tend to dwell more on their lines, pottering around and being disinclined to push on.

Hounds that lack drive are very difficult to read and are usually quite willing to stop work or change onto another line should the handler misdirect them. Lacking concentration and confidence, they frequently look to the handler for reassurance, are distracted by sights and sounds around, urinate frequently and generally look bored. Lines at trials are hot compared with a real situation. If a hound finds great difficulty in working out a line that is only an hour cold, he is unlikely to be any good when asked to follow a trail six or more hours cold.

A really keen hound, on the other hand, is difficult to lift and will try to return to a line if asked to cast in the wrong direction. He will display that relentless determination and persistence that is characteristic of the breed. However, drive should not be confused with speed. There are many hounds which can maintain a good speed for short distances, only to stop suddenly when they get away from their handlers or when they hit a difficult patch. The hound with drive will work enthusiastically, if slowly, even when the scent is poor.

Accuracy

Accuracy is also important: not only does the scent of the runner stay in the footsteps where he has walked, but scent particles also drop from him and are blown some distance from the line by the wind. These particles accumulate downwind of the line, on the ground or catching in a hedge, rather as light fluff dropped would tend to blow downwind and catch in twigs. Young hounds are often confused by the drifted scent, they find patches and assume that the line is there, but when the scent peters out they are at a loss to know where to look for it. Experienced hounds will bring themselves up to the wind and follow the footsteps more accurately.

If the runner is standing upwind at the end of the line it is quite possible for the hound to wind-scent him from a considerable distance. The hound's behaviour will be quite different then from when following the track: he will throw his head up and sniff the air, then work his way towards the runner with his head up, usually on a swinging line as the scent blows unevenly towards him. He may miss out part of the track in this way, but should not be penalised for it; after all, it is not his fault that the line has been arranged so that the runner is upwind.

Luke hot on the trail!

The judge should be careful not to foil the line, especially in a following wind, as the scent of a human and a sweaty horse may obliterate the runner's scent on a poor day.

Speed

Speed of working is, of course, a criterion to be considered, although it should by no means be given priority. Good hounds with drive will usually work as fast as the scenting conditions will allow, but they are also accurate. Older hounds will usually work their lines slower than young hounds, and should not be penalised for it, providing they show the necessary drive and do not waste time. If a hound is handled on a leash, of course, his speed is dependent upon his handler.

Hounds should settle quickly to the line and not go dashing about overenthusiastically. Many years ago I assisted in a Novice Stake. One of the hounds was extremely fast, he scampered straight down a hedge, through a gate, along another hedge, another gate, along a river edge to his runner. His handler was very disappointed to find that he had not won a prize, until it was explained that the hound had not hunted the line at all, but had followed the hedges. He touched the line only at the gates, the line going out in wide loops from the flags, between the gates and wide from the river bank. He never really settled at all to the line, and came upon his runner more by luck than anything else.

Casting

Should the hound overshoot a turn, he should be almost instantly aware that he has run out of scent and turn back to pick it up again. A hound that runs on even though the scent is no longer there should be penalised. If the hound comes to a check he should show his ability to cast himself properly. Some hounds, particularly youngsters or ones that have been overhandled, will look to their handler to put them right when they run out of scent; good hounds will work methodically to regain their lines themselves.

A hound should be easy to read, and this is never so important as when the line is temporarily lost. It should be seen instantly when the hound regains the scent, by the sudden stop as he crosses the track, the feathering of his stern and the sudden excitement which is visible throughout his body – he positively vibrates. It is difficult to describe a good hound when he suddenly comes across the scent he is searching for. It could be likened to the triumph a child shows when he finds the piece of a jigsaw puzzle that has eluded him. A good hound casting will be oblivious to his surroundings and not until he has searched really hard and fruitlessly will he look to his handler for assistance.

Obstacles

Hounds must be able to negotiate obstacles such as fences, hedges, gates, walls and water, and should clearly mark those that the runner has touched. A hound that has to be helped through or over reasonable obstacles should be penalised, particularly if he makes no effort to negotiate them himself. These remarks should of course be tempered with common sense, a bloodhound is a heavy animal and should not be expected to leap effortlessly about like a terrier, but he should at least try to get over, through or round any obstacle even if it is impossibly high. A good hound will sometimes scream with frustration when he cannot get over a fence.

WT Ch. Sanguine Abingerwood Tinsel marks a gate where the runner has crossed.

Confidence

Many hounds will not go on without their handlers. This may or may not be a fault. Some hounds simply wait for the slower member of the team to catch up in a kindly sort of way, while others, however, clearly lose confidence when they are alone, and should be penalised. In a real situation, of course, the hound would either be worked in harness or the scent would be so stale that the handler would have no difficulty in keeping up with him.

Speaking

Most judges appreciate a good voice, properly used, but penalise a hound that babbles or speaks when he is not on the line. If the hound speaks, he should do so only when he has the scent. He should remain silent when casting, until he picks up the line again, when he can throw his tongue and move forward. A very few judges prefer a hound to remain silent. This follows the theory that if you were following a criminal you would not want to give advance warning of your presence by a baying hound. This would certainly be true if you were anticipating a terrorist ambush, but in most cases, the sound of a baying bloodhound approaching would make a fugitive break cover and run for it, when he would be easily caught in the open. As for lost children being frightened by hound music, personally, if I was lost on a moor, I would be only too delighted to hear a sound that showed someone was looking for me!

Certainly a hound using his voice properly is very helpful in trials, as it shows clearly when he is on the line, whether in sight of his handler or not, and the voice makes it much easier for hound and handler to work as a team. A handler can cut corners and catch up with a fast hound if he can hear where he is.

Identification

At the end of the line, a hound should identify his runner. This is particularly important in the Senior Stake, where, unless the hound picks his runner from a group of three to the judges satisfaction, he cannot be considered for the Kennel Club Working Trial Certificate. Whatever method he has been trained to use for identification, whether the classic placing of forepaws on the runner's shoulders, waving the stern or staring, the hound in any stake should be able to demonstrate clearly to the judge that he has found his quarry.

The Handler

The handler plays an important part in a hound's work, although only as the back-up man in the team. It should be clear throughout the line that the hound is doing the actual hunting and is not relying on the handler for making progress. The handler should give the hound encouragement and if he has not completed his cast should give him assistance by trying him in a quarter he has not checked or urging him forward to fresh ground. However, the hound should always be the leader of the team, the handler following him, not the other way round!

Handlers can also get information from the ground itself, footsteps, crushed vegetation etc., and whilst this is helpful to them so that they can cheer their hounds on with that much more confidence, the hound should also be seen to be working the line for himself.

Judges should also be very careful that they do not inadvertently give assistance and information to the handler by their behaviour. Wily handlers keep one eye glued on the judge, and notice quickly if he has stopped following, is facing in any particular direction or taking a short cut. A judge should be careful, therefore, at a check that he does not give the game away unintentionally.

I have to admit that a good deal of quiet amusement can be gained from some handlers' reliance on a judge. On one occasion when I was judging a stake, I noticed that at the first check the handler took his hound to the left to cast. My horse just happened to be facing that direction at the time. At the next check I noticed the gimlet eye and experimentally turned my horse to the right. The handler immediately cast in that direction. After that it was quite amusing to see how the handler could be persuaded to cast his hound, simply by turning my horse! I don't think this was really unfair, as the handler should have been watching his

Boravin Fusilier handled by Margaret Lowe, finding his quarry S. Selman, on an Intermediate line. Sussex, autumn 1979.

WT Ch. Sanguine Saintly, handled by Henry Edwards.

hound, not my horse, and the observation was so blatant I just could not resist it.

Judges should not give advice to a handler unless it is specifically requested. In the Senior Stake, advice given will prevent the award of a Kennel Club Working Trial Certificate, and throughout the stakes, handlers prefer to work their hounds themselves without help. It can be very frustrating, however, to watch a handler pushing his hound in the wrong direction without interfering, especially if the hound doesn't want to go there. You must wait until they are both so far off the line, and clearly not hunting, that there is no chance of their regaining it without help. Of course there may be instances when they must be called off because they are approaching forbidden territory or some danger. I do not think they should be called off because they are approaching another line if the hound is working and has shown no signs of changing. There are usually crossed lines on a trials area, and this will only be another crossing. The judge can note the spot carefully and make allowances, if he thinks fit, for the other hound.

Style

The final consideration in judging is style, that elusive quality that makes a hound a pleasure to watch. It is really a combination of factors, drive being the most dominant and usually the best hound of the day shows plenty of style. However, it can happen that an unimpressive hound works his line out and gets to his runner better than the hounds showing more style. In this case, the ability to find the quarry should be given more weight than the style in which it was done. Although most judges do not like giving a prize to an uninteresting hound, if he has hunted the line without being pushed round it by his handler, he must be considered.

Awarding Prizes

At the end of the day the judge will be expected to make his decisions, give out prizes and explain his reasons to the competitors. He will probably find that one, or possibly two or three hounds have stood out from the rest, and their work has given him real pleasure. If he has had to leave any hounds to his assistants because of lack of time, he should check with them as to the rest of the line. Although a hound that did not impress him in the time he spent with it will be unlikely to improve much later, he could find that a hound that seemed good has made a glaring mistake which will have put it out of the running.

It is important to remember that any prize won should be earned. The hounds are not only competing against each other but against an imaginary standard, and if the best hounds of the day do not come up to the judge's expectations, he should withhold prizes. The competitors also prefer to know that any prizes they win are truly deserved.

Another reason for withholding prizes is that a first prize in a stake automatically takes the hound out of that stake and into the next, more difficult one. It stands to reason that if, in the judge's opinion, the hound is not yet up to the work asked of him, he will not be able to compete favourably doing something more difficult, so he should stay in his present stake until he is more proficient.

When all the hounds have worked their lines, the judge has made his decisions and marked the prize cards, he will be expected to give a resumé of the day's work, and later, a written report. There is a real interest in the reasons for his results, as few spectators will have seen all the lines in their entirety. After the formal prizegiving, there is usually time for the judge to have a discussion with the competitors over a relaxed drink – he will have earned it.

It is usual, and most helpful, for the judge to send a written report to the organiser at a later date, which can be printed in the organising society's newsletter and which establishes an accurate record of events of the day's hunting.'

The Quarry

The quarry at bloodhound working trials is, of course, a human 'runner'. Some people, who know nothing about trials, shudder at the idea of being asked to be a quarry for bloodhounds, picturing themselves running, exhausted over the fields with a baying hound at their heels! In fact, nothing could be further from the reality of the situation; walking a line is a peaceful and most enjoyable pastime.

Trials in Britain are held in spring and autumn when there are few people around and the countryside is often at its most beautiful. In spring, the trees, not yet in full bloom, impose a grey-green tinge on the landscape and new life abounds in the fields and hedgerows. On the other hand, autumn contains a stillness and beauty all of its own; the landscape tinged with the browns, golds and greens of the remains of the dense summer foliage.

Providing the weather is reasonable, nothing could be more pleasant than a quiet, solitary walk across this colourful countryside with only farm stock and wildlife for company. On a Senior Stake you may have to walk for about an hour and a half without seeing anyone except perhaps an occasional farm worker.

Quite often, trials are held on private land not normally open to the general public. To walk a line over this type of country is a rare opportunity to observe animals and birds which are largely undisturbed throughout the year. Foxes and deer are quite commonly seen, and some runners have even encountered badgers.

The weather plays a critical role in the enjoyment of walking a line; the British weather in autumn and spring is so notoriously unpredictable. I have walked lines in all sorts of conditions: heatwave, snow, hail, rain and bitterly cold winds. In many cases one would have thought that there was no chance of any scent staying. On one occasion, after a week of continuous downpour, the rain was so heavy that water was cascading down the hillside leaving very little ground above a rushing torrent. It is incredible that scent could be left behind under such conditions, but it invariably is, even if only in patches.

Apart from the pleasure to be had from simply walking over the land, there is a great deal of satisfaction to be gained from walking the line accurately, using the map and orienteering through difficult country.

If you are asked to walk a line at a working trial, there are certain disciplines to bear in mind. These simply help to ensure that all the hounds entered have a reasonably equal chance.

1. Do not wear gum boots. Some competitors might feel that this makes an unfair disadvantage because the boots do not emit scent in the same way as leather or porous footwear. Personally I feel that this point is debatable, but it is best to avoid any arguments on this score.

2. Never retrace your footsteps. This could cause a hound to spend a great deal of time working out an unnecessary problem, especially in bad scenting conditions.

If you realise that you have taken the wrong route:

3. Do not try to regain the line by walking along a metalled road. Not only does this make scenting difficult but it is also extremely dangerous.

4. Try to aim for the correct end of the line keeping the distance as close as possible to the original. Always remember to correct the map and return it to the judge as soon as you finish so that he can study it before the hound is laid on.

Let us imagine that you have been asked to walk a typical Senior line three miles in length, across open country. The hound will be laid on two hours after you have set out. Make sure that you arrive wearing suitable waterproof clothing and strong footwear and are armed with a smeller.

First you are given instructions and a map showing the line. It is imperative to study this map closely before setting out. However, one word of warning here: many of the maps used were published over twenty years ago and although major alterations to the land that have occurred should have been marked by the organiser, the shape of fields, position of hedges, buildings, plantations etc. could well have changed.

Particular features to note when studying the map initially are the contours and obvious landmarks such as pylons, roads, railway lines, streams and farm buildings. These will all help in following the line accurately.

You would probably then be driven to the start of the line and given two white flags, each on a separate stake about 18 in. (45 cm) long. Onto one of these you tie a piece of clothing containing your scent. Some people use a pocket handkerchief, others use the smelliest sock they own. Having consulted the map and decided the direction you are to follow, you stick the flag with the smeller attached in the ground and set off. After about twenty paces you stick the second flag in the ground. The two flags help the handler to settle his hound onto the scent at the start. The Bloodhound Club, however, consider the practice of using a second flag unnecessary for a Senior Stake and dispense with it.

Of course, it should be clearly understood that at no time is anything dragged along the ground to create a stronger scent, nor are artificial means (e.g. aniseed etc.) used to help the hound.

There are a variety of problems encountered on the average line but the most important thing to remember is that the map must be followed as closely as possible. Do not be tempted to put in an extra obstacle because you feel that the hound might find it amusing to sort out, and, by the same token, do not try to be kind to the hound and handler by deliberately leaving chunks of mud on gates and fences showing where you have crossed. Of course, when you have climbed a fence and mud is accidentally left behind that is quite in the order of the sport and there is no need to carefully expunge all traces.

Cattle are always a problem as they do like to involve themselves in whatever is going on, especially in spring when they have been let out after a winter under cover. Horses are often also a problem, galloping around from one end of a field to the other.

A major problem for any runner is created by mist or fog. This is especially common on open moorland and can come down very quickly obliterating distant – and even near – landmarks and making navigation very difficult. It is always a good idea to carry a compass in case of fog, or even heavy rain. On one occasion on Exmoor, the mist was so thick that we lost the runner, the hound, the handler and the judge with his two assistants! Fortunately this state of affairs does not occur too often.

Moorland is also noted for its bogs and although few of them are actual killers, it is very unpleasant to sink into them. In places such as the New Forest, where there are wild ponies, it is a good idea to look out for droppings, as the ponies know the bad bogs and it is safe to assume that if the ground has taken their weight, it is safe for you to venture over.

To sum up, line walking can be a most enjoyable experience but the most important thing to remember is to have complete honesty. Anyone can misread a map or the country and most of us have done it on more than one occasion. It is nothing to be embarrassed about, so if you get lost, say so, otherwise it is unfair to all concerned, and in the end it is the hound which will prove the point.

The Mystery of Scent

Scent is a fascinating but little understood subject and I am not going to profess a full comprehension of it – nobody can do that. There are a great many theories on scent and scenting conditions and I present some of these here to try and give a picture of the skill required to follow a scent.

The scent followed by hounds is made up of a variety of odours and is affected by many factors. It is believed that a hound can form a 'scent picture' – in the same way that we recognise shapes and colours – and interprets this to give the information required.

Basically, the hound detects two sources of scent: body scent (the individual scent of the runner) and foot-tread scent (given off as a result of crushing insects and vegetation underfoot). Both of these are affected by environmental conditions and either remain on the ground (ground scent) or are blown like smoke downwind (wind scent).

In the absence of environmental influences, the body scent would fall to the ground as minute globules of vapour (for want of a better word) in a pyramid-type shape. However, in a natural situation the way in which it falls is affected by wind, temperature and humidity and I believe that these influences result in a layering effect as shown on p. 143. The scent will usually be strongest at one level and distributed in lesser strengths on the other levels. Very often a hound is seen hunting with its head up in the air – 'hunting the breast-high scent'.

Bobbie Edwards and WT Ch. Sanguine Abingerwood Tinsel.

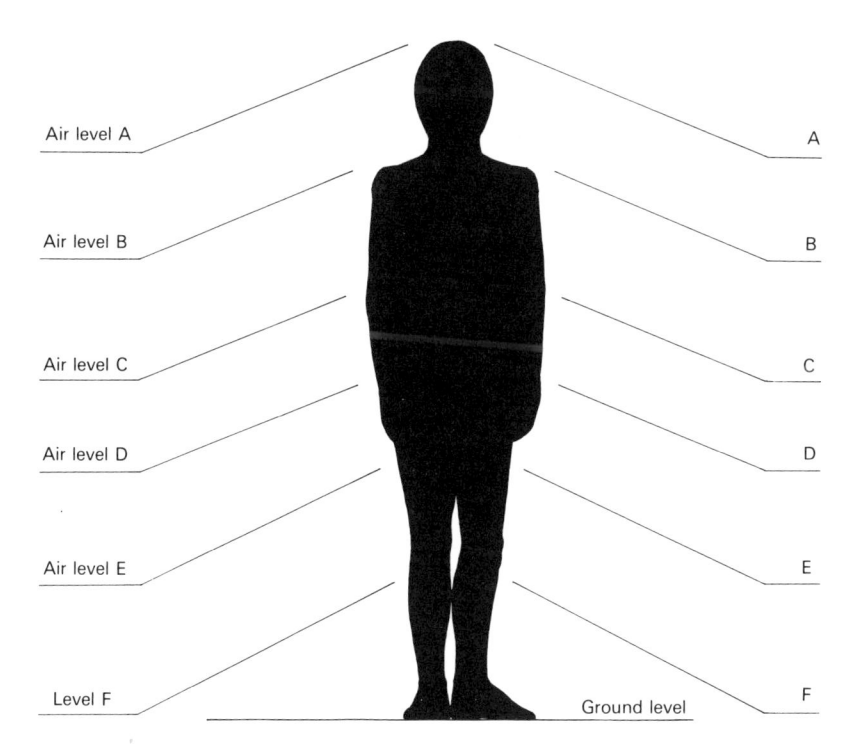

Air level A		A
Air level B		B
Air level C		C
Air level D		D
Air level E		E
Level F	Ground level	F

Scent falling from the body tends to form layers.

Foot-tread scent is influenced by the type of soil, the amount and type of vegetation, chemical fertilisers and whether the soil has been disturbed recently, among other things.

Temperature has a strong effect on general scenting conditions. If the ground is warmer than the air above it, then the scent will rise and good scenting conditions should result. Conversely, if the air is warmer than the soil or is at roughly the same temperature, then the scent will be poor. Hunting in hot weather is therefore best confined to early morning or late evening.

Wind will obviously blow scent away from the line and will often cause it to build up against obstacles such as hedges or buildings. In a strong wind you will often see hounds hunting well but at a considerable distance downwind from the actual line. This proves without doubt that scent can be carried on the wind for some distance. I would also suggest that scent blown from the body will most likely disappear quicker than that of the foot tread, but while body scent remains, it may well be stronger for the hound to follow.

I do not believe that the porosity of the footwear worn by a runner has any great influence on scent. Even when a line has been walked by a runner wearing rubber boots, a hound has no difficulty in following the scent.

Another common belief is that scent is obliterated by water. A hunted man is supposed to be able to throw the hound simply by walking through a stream or pond. This theory has been disproved so often that it is strange to find it still suggested. On one occasion, when hunting my first bloodhound, Sanguine Sable, the line was interrupted by a river about 10 yd (9 m) across but only about 18 in. (46 cm) deep. The hound waded straight over to the other side and cast around until he picked up some drifting scent, then he crossed back to the bank on which I stood and found more scent. Gradually progressing down the river he crossed from bank to bank picking up scent on either side until he finally came to the point, some 50 yd (45 m) downstream, where the runner had left the river and off he went.

Despite all the theories about scent, the one thing that can be said with certainty is that it is unpredictable. On some days you can be hunting in lush pastureland and there is no scent at all but you cross to bare plough and the hound has no difficulty whatsoever.

Above all else, the ability of the hound to detect scent under all conditions never fails to amaze and mystify me. At one trial I remember a senior hound was started on a line on dry plough in a very exposed area. A gale force wind was blasting across the country and had been blowing since the runner set out two hours previously. The hound's nose almost dug up the soil in an attempt to find the scent. He went up and down between the flags three or four times without success, working furiously. Suddenly he stopped in his tracks, his nose motionless in contact with the ground, the rest of his body quivering like a coiled spring, his stern threshing wildly from side to side. He threw his tongue with excitement, catapulted himself forward a few paces, stopped

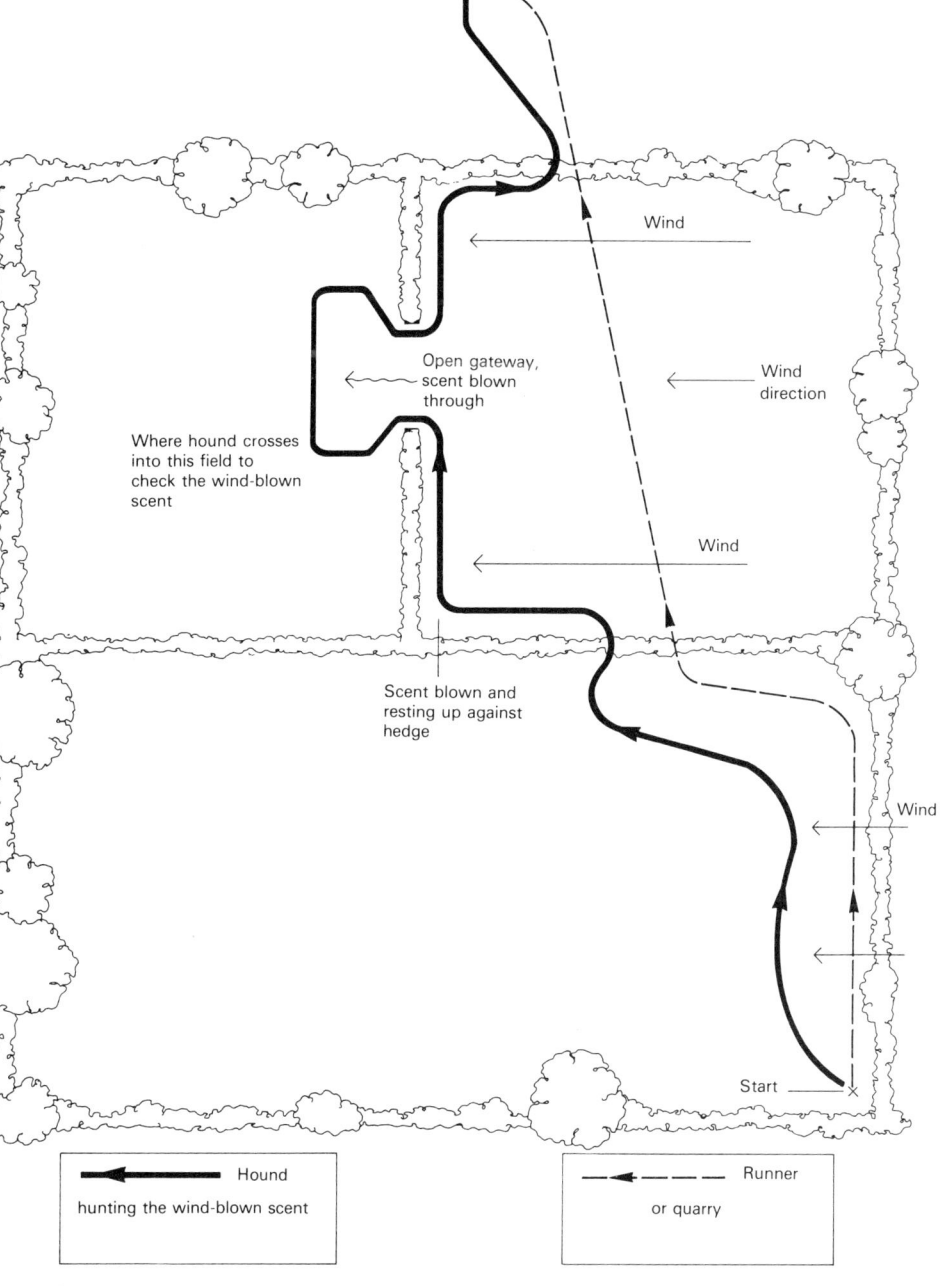

Scent will be blown downwind to a varying extent, dependent on the terrain and barriers, such as hedges, against which it tends to accumulate.

again, then rushed forward again. He repeated this procedure several times, each time following the direction of the line. Eventually he knew that he had got the line and continued on at a great pace towards the far corner of the field, went through a gap in the hedge and was gone, his handler straining to catch up in vain.

Moments such as this, when it seems that there is no possibility that any scent could remain and yet the hound finds some, are, to me, the most rewarding of all to watch.

A Senior Line

Having considered the various elements that go towards making successful bloodhound trials possible, I illustrate the discussion with an example of a Senior line.

This line resulted in the awarding of a Kennel Club Working Trial Certificate to Sanguine Saturn, owned by Mr and Mrs H. H. Edwards and hunted by Mrs Bobbie Edwards on the Cottesbrooke Estate, Leicestershire, England in the spring of 1978. It is described here from the point of view of the runner (Mrs Jane Crease) and the handler (Mrs Bobbie Edwards).

The Runner

> One of the fascinating things about hunting bloodhounds is the fillip it can give to one's normal memories of places and things. To hunt over a piece of country, or to be hunted over it, very often means that one can totally recall its physical characteristics – the growing crops, the state of the ground, the weather and so on. Superimposed on all of this is the marvellous picture of a bloodhound, casting forward and then driving on, speaking to the line and then turning, perhaps into the wind to catch even the smallest snatches of scent.
>
> Having walked the winning line on this particular occasion, I can still see the hound hunting up to my feet at the finish, the trail of my footsteps clearly marked in the winter wheat and the hound deviating only inches from it on running in. The line was over arable land, mainly spring-sown corn, but with a good stretch of winter wheat which was six inches or so high. Some of the land had only just been sown and had been ploughed in thick ridges.

The line [line 5 on the map] started in a field of grass, carried on through a narrow covert, and then went sharply downhill to some lush growth of winter wheat where it made a sharp curve. While standing on the hill watching the hound it was possible to see the track I had made in the wheat where I had walked and the hound hunting almost exactly on the same line. After the sharp curve it continued uphill, crossed a tricky farm track on the way to a windswept hillside with newly sown corn coming through. It then went across the hedge and past a field of grazing sheep behind some netting. Then through another big right-handed loop, along the line of an old hedge which had been grubbed out and burnt – the old charred stumps sticking out of the ground – and back through some really heavy ridged plough. Only the final field had much in the way of growth on this section of the line – winter wheat again.

Watching a hound hunt a line you have walked is one of the most instructive ways to learn about hound work. You know where you went, you see where the hound has owned the line and you learn much about the tricks that the weather and scent can play. A close hunting hound can often hunt along in the runner's footprints – as this one did – and will only acknowledge the actual ground scent. The reward is at the end: the hound hunting right up to the runner's feet, oblivious of his presence until the last yard or so.

The Handler

Saturn's line, the second of the day, started at 10.30 a.m. on a good grass field. I knew she was full of enthusiasm and confidence that morning, although I had misgivings as the previous hound had put up a first rate performance which would be hard to beat. Saturn went up to the flag (only one on a Senior Stake), cast quickly round it and was off, speaking with great joy. I expected her to slow down after the first flush of enthusiasm, but she maintained her speed to the top of the field, took a sharp left turn through the end of the narrow wood and raced off across the winter wheat.

I took some time getting through two fences, and when I next saw her she was way off down by the stream, still speaking joyously and accompanied by Major Borwick and his horse. As I ran down,

Overleaf: Aerial photograph of the Cottesbrooke Estate, Leicestershire, showing the land used for five lines on the second day of the Senior Stake, Bloodhound Club Trials, spring 1978. Each line (labelled S for start and F for finish) is 3 miles long.

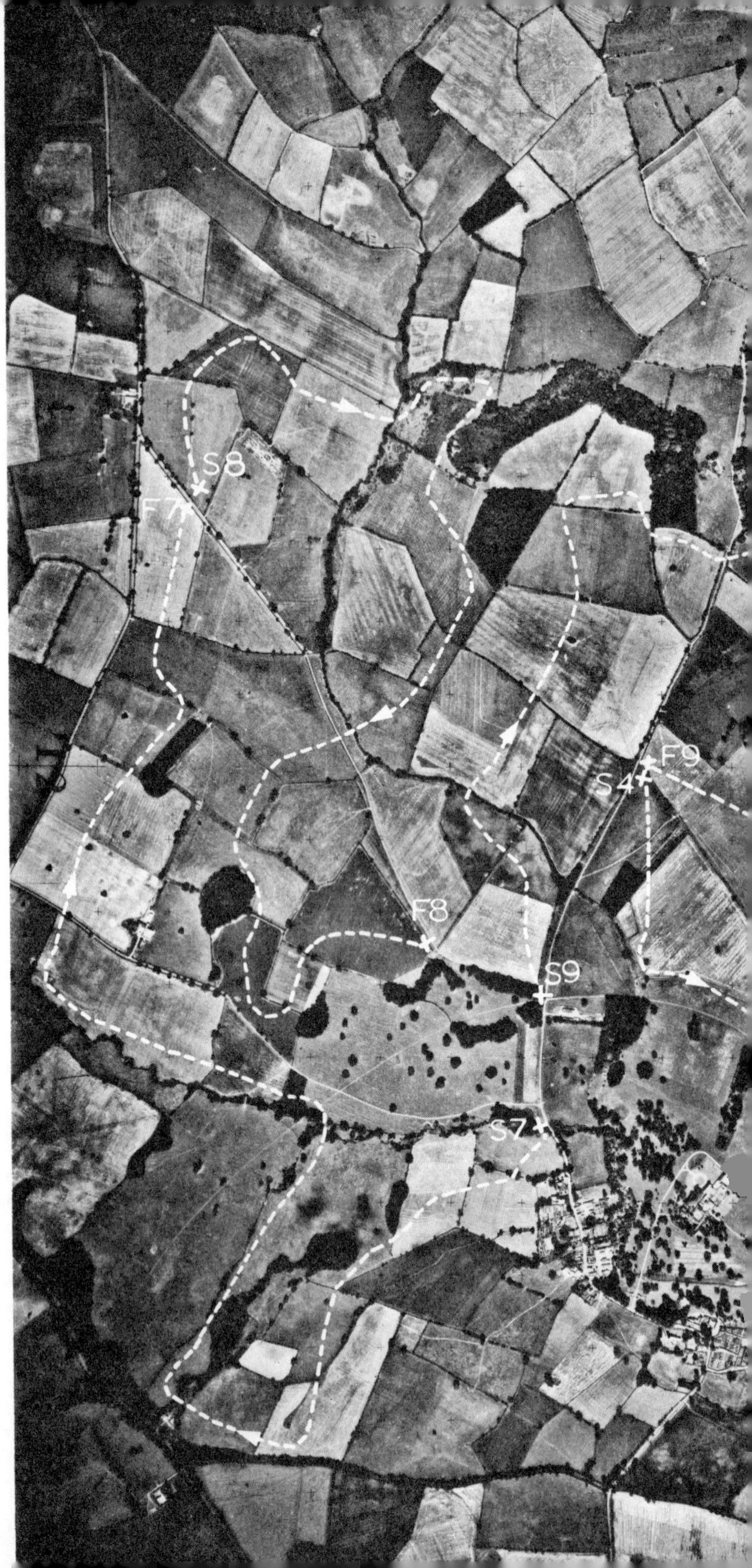

S8
F7
F9
S4
F8
S9
S7

S5
F4

F5

Aerial photograph showing the Senior line (number 5) described here by the runner (Jane Crease) and the handler (Bobbie Edwards).

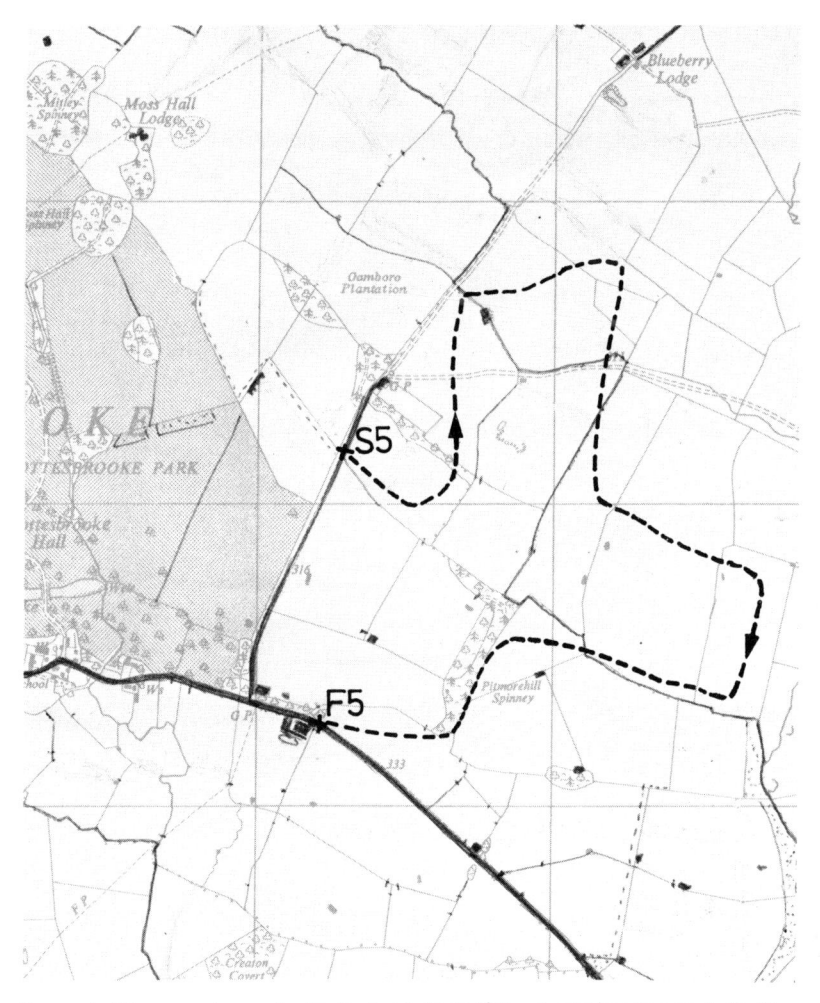

Segment of the runner's map for Senior line 5. Scale 2½ in. = 1 mile (modern equivalent is 1:25,000).

she turned right, and, still accompanied by the horse now galloping, hunted on along the strip fields. I was faced with a dilemma: should I run after her, it seemed most unlikely that I could catch up, but if on the line I could help her if she got into difficulties; or should I guess where the line might turn back and take a short cut down there. I chose the latter course of action and ran as fast as I could, hoping she would not turn back.

I met her where she was at a temporary check by a difficult hedge. She got through the hedge, and on to a heavily foiled track where the scent was very difficult because of sheep and farm work, which caused considerable casting, but after some time she went over the sheep wire fence and into a field of rolled plough which had been recently fertilised. She worked up this long field with care, speaking whenever she hit the line. At the top there was a sharp turn left along the fence where we had an audience of several hundred sheep gazing across at us with interest. She was then off across the next two fields to a shed with a difficult hedge crossing before it and a track. A momentary hesitation here, then on, a right turn along the next field and another right turn at the boundary hedge.

Since I had caught up with her we had been alone, Major Borwick having been wired in by the stream and Sergeant Yeandle and his followers remaining up on high ground on our right. However, at this point Major Borwick and his steamy horse caught up and accompanied us for the rest of the line. We went a fair way along the boundary hedge, the line being difficult here as tractors had created a hard path. In the corner we came to a very difficult wire and twig fence which Saturn found very frustrating and difficult to get through as there was no clear jump, but after two or three attempts and a lot of frustrated noise, she cleared it and raced on past a small shed, and on to the corner of the wood. She worked round this rather more slowly, again the ground here was much used, and came out into the final field of winter wheat. The better scent on this ground gave her another burst of speed, and she went in confidently to where her runner and two others were forming an identification parade, leaning against a rail fence. Without hesitation she went up to her runner, clearly thanked her for walking such an enjoyable line, and, after checking to see that I was still with her and all right (I was with her but virtually speechless as the speed had been killing), she ducked under the fence and trotted through the crowd, clearly pleased with herself. The time was about forty-five minutes.

There was really very little I could say about the line, because she hunted it in copybook fashion, and too fast for me to enjoy the scenery or be more than dimly aware of my surroundings. Where the scent was good she went very fast, where it was poor she worked slowly and carefully, following the footsteps whenever I could see them exactly, and working out the heavily foiled parts diligently until she could regain the line. I knew to an inch exactly where the runner went, and how she had crossed all the obstacles on the line – Saturn marked each place where the runner's hand or foot had touched the wire or branches. She spoke all the way except when she had temporarily run out of scent, which was lucky for me as I knew exactly what she was doing although sometimes she was out of sight. She never lost her drive or confidence, in spite of the fact that for the last half of the line I was so out of breath I had practically nothing left to cheer her on! How I wished I could have borrowed Major Borwick's horse!

5
Comments from Experienced Huntsmen

The following accounts are by those who have had considerable experience hunting bloodhounds in the field. It is their opinion that I respect and hope that their comments will prove to be a lasting and valuable contribution to the working bloodhound in years to come.

Reg R. Wright M.H., Master of the North Warwickshire Bloodhounds

I have known Reg since I first became interested in bloodhounds. A colourful character in hunting circles, Reg's career spans a considerable period of time and he has been involved in many forms of hunting. Starting traditionally, with foxhounds, he later developed a keen interest in beagles, which he hunted for about sixteen seasons, and ultimately, bloodhounds, in which he has been actively interested for over twenty years. Reg talked to me about his experiences and views:

> With foxhunting, you have to first find your fox; with beagles you have to first find your hare; but with bloodhounds your quarry is already laid on. You waste no time in having to draw a fox either in woods or fields.
> I believe that essential features for today's working bloodhound are speed and stamina. Unfortunately, it became obvious to some of us a few years ago, that these qualities were becoming rarer, and

Mr and Mrs Reg R. Wright and the North Warwickshire Bloodhounds.

in order to remedy this, both Eric Furness, who owned the Peak Bloodhounds, and I decided to try outcrossing.

Eric managed to obtain two Dumfriesshire foxhound bitches from Sir Rupert Buchanan-Jardine which he then used to cross with his pure-bred bloodhounds. Years later, when Eric gave up his hounds he let me have two half Dumfriesshire foxhound bitches called Cautious and Charming, both of which had been crossed with his pure-bred bloodhound. It was noticeable that they did not have the ear of the pure bloodhound.

In my outcross, I used a Kendall otterhound bitch which I put to one of my pure-bred bloodhounds. This cross resulted in a much faster animal.

It was my intention, as it was Eric's, to try and achieve a more functional hound than that which the then bloodhound had, we felt, degenerated into. However, one major problem which finally decided us on this course of action was that, between us, we had lost six hounds with bloat. As far as I know, none of the outcrosses has been a victim of bloat.

The hounds hunted in Eric's country in Derbyshire have to be able to jump a hundred or so stone walls in a day – that's a lot of walls – and they must be able to see them before they get to them. It is essential for the hounds to be able to jump, or the pack becomes spread out, some in one field and some in the next. This prevents you riding up with the horses and makes the whole hunt far too dispersed.

The distances that hounds must travel in Derbyshire make plenty of stamina essential. On one occasion with Eric, the runner had inadvertently walked nine miles and the hounds just kept going. You must remember that these hounds were very fast and it would take a good horse to stay with them. Now, I consider that my own hounds are as fast as foxhounds, and, I believe, are, if anything, a little faster than Eric's were because, unlike Eric who had bred back to the bloodhound, I brought my otterhound-cross-bloodhound back to my bloodhound-cross-foxhound. You see, I brought these two together, whereas Eric kept going back and choosing a pure-bred bloodhound. I really had the benefit passed on to me from Eric getting these two hounds from Sir Rupert Buchanan-Jardine and the fact that I originally had the two otterhound crosses from Wales, and so I was lucky in that respect. More recently I have the Welsh foxhound and English foxhound and intend to keep some puppies out of each, which means I will still have outcross and am able to keep both lines going.

My hounds are not necessarily as tall as some of the showhounds and although I like a tallish, rangy dog, as long as he is not too lightly built, there is a limit to its height for its purpose. It is the same with horses; you don't want a long backed horse built like a battleship to jump. You want a hound to be like a horse (imagine if you had to put a saddle on him): he wants a lot in front and not a lot behind. As a matter of fact, he has to do the same job, as horse and hound have to cover the same ground.

When I used to have the beagles and bassetts, someone once remarked to me, 'They are an odd lot, Reg.'

I said, 'Yes, they are. But they are a bloody odder lot that follow!'

A glaring fault with today's bloodhounds is bad eyes. A good, clean eye is a feature that I think is vital in a hound. When hunting, a hound must be able to see where it is going, especially when it is having to jump dry stone walls and sheep wire. At the pace some of them travel, they would dash their brains out if they hit one of those walls badly.

Feet are another problem area with bloodhounds. A foxhound's feet are neat and well knuckled, unlike the bloodhound's, and if a hound has bad feet, it follows that it usually has a bad pastern and poor joints. Incidentally, I never cut the dew claws off my bloodhounds because it gives them that little bit more help in clearing a wall or fence. In all my years of hunting bloodhounds I have never known one to tear.

I believe that it is useful for hounds to have a rangy frame though not too light. Tall hounds are good in that they can pace, but they should not be too long. You will notice that there are some terrible movers amongst bloodhounds today, but in the ones that Eric Furness and I bred, the hind leg does not go under – it is straighter – with most of the bloodhounds it goes under. By outcrossing selectively we have done away with that. You will also notice the lack of bend of stifle in most bloodhounds. Bend of stifle is essential for powerful drive; good hounds must have hind legs nearer to those of a hare in order to propel them along.

You see, you have to be careful when criticising a hound's make-up. I once knew one bitch which was knuckled up – she would sit there at the meet and you could see her joint give quite

The North Warwickshire Bloodhound Pack identifies its quarry.

obviously. But that hound never missed a day's hunting. So one has to be careful in suggesting that they cannot do the job.

If you look at some of the old photographs of bloodhounds from the last century, they do not look much like today's bloodhound; they are more like the English foxhound. I believe that we have, with many of today's bloodhounds, got too far away from what he is supposed to be.

Naturally, my own interest has also taken into account the bloodhound trials where I had some success and which I have thoroughly enjoyed. In fact, I was one of the instigators responsible for starting up the Bloodhound Club again after it had ceased to function.

You will, of course, be familiar with the derivation of the title of your book, which is the long established reference made by bloodhound enthusiasts towards hunting human scent, 'hunting the clean boot'. Now I disagree with the theory that scent only works through the soles of your boots. It is body scent, and how it lies, and I will argue with anybody on that question. It is something science has not interfered with yet and I suggest never will. My theory is that scent lies in layers. You will have noticed that some hounds will never put their noses on the ground. In my opinion it rises to a certain level and stops at that level. Also, I believe it falls from the body from the head downwards, also forming in layers. This is why I think that the argument against the wearing of Wellington boots at trials is irrelevant.

Another point to bear in mind is that some folks smell more to hounds than others. I do not know whether you have noticed it, but hounds tend to win at trials on particular people.

The absorbing thing about hunting and scent is that it is unpredictable. Although it is accepted that there are many pointers to either a good or a bad scent, they are not infallible indicators. If it is a clear morning you sometimes find that it is not a good scenting day; but there are many exceptions to this rule. Nothing is certain with scent.

I remember one occasion when I was hunting with Eric. We got up in the morning only to find that after a very cold night, it was a very frosty morning. 'That's done it!' I said, 'There'll be a terrible scent.' However, they had got hold of an enthusiastic runner – I believe he was a local school teacher – and they sent him about five miles, not more. None of us thought that it would be very good, but they laid the hounds on (this was Eric's pack) and they went away like the devil. Thirty-seven horses started, and at the end of the line there were only thirteen. They just did not have the stamina to keep going up the long banks which were over very rough, heavy ground.

It is an interesting point that on some days we would try hunting the bloodhounds to see what sort of scent there was for the beagles. We have known a bad scenting day for the beagles, then come back, run a line for the bloodhounds and they have gone a tremendous pace. The fact is I have never had a bad day with the bloodhounds. Bad scenting, yes, but never a dull time.

It is worth remembering in a competitive situation such as at the trials that it is the hound who is hunting and the handler who tracks. There is no point relying implicitly on the chap who has given you a map, since he may well have misread it, or in fact, cannot read it at all. The best advice is to learn to read maps and rely on the nose and intelligence of the hound. I used to attend many trials as a handler, reading the country and my hound, noticing whether there was broken foliage, footprints, or

Reg R. Wright M.H. and hound at bloodhound working trials.

disturbance of stock and wildlife suggesting that someone had passed that way. In fact, they even called me the 'Red Indian', and I thoroughly enjoyed hunting a single hound.

I have one boast, and that is not losing my temper. I can honestly say that I never lose my temper when I am hunting bloodhounds, because if you do you automatically conduct it to them. They will detect the raising of your voice immediately. I have never cussed a whipper-in, or a member of the field and I believe this to be very important.

When judging working trials, I tend to place hounds in order of merit as they appear, but when I think one does better, I move him up. That is where a hound with a voice scores that extra bit of something and, of course, you, as a handler, have that extra bit to play with.

Once I remember when I was hunting my pack, I had been asked to put on a show with the bloodhounds in the Belvoir Vale. They were all hunting people and we had quite a field following. Anyway, away they went. When two foxes and a hare got up right on the line, those folks thought they were going to have a fox hunt.

The North Warwickshire Pack on its way back to kennels.

But those hounds never changed. I was as proud of them as any time I have ever been.

There is much that one can suggest to beginners in taking up this sport, but remember there is no quick answer for understanding its many puzzles, both from the point of view of hounds and scent. But learn patience with yourself, your hounds and others and you will enjoy a most rewarding sport in the countryside.

David L. Kingsberry M.R.C.V.S.

David is an experienced handler whom I have admired for many years.

This is written by an amateur for the amateur in the hope that some of my ideas may be of use in training a bloodhound to hunt successfully at bloodhound working trials.

Having started with bloodhounds with a background of ordinary working trials and obedience work, as opposed to the hunting field, I was first impressed by the fact that the bloodhound has the ability to track over different types of surface, be it grass or concrete, without the apparent difficulty usually found with other breeds. It was not until later, that a chance remark by the late Sergeant Harry Darbyshire, who was largely responsible for training the first police dogs after the war with the Surrey Constabulary and who owned a tracking bloodhound himself, made me realise that bloodhounds *hunt* whereas other breeds of working dog have to be taught to *track*.

A bloodhound hunts naturally and it is for its owner to guide it and so train it to hunt man and to stick to one particular person, namely the tracklayer or runner, at a time.

In my view it is essential to start bloodhounds tracking when they are young: three month old puppies will hunt to find their owners if so encouraged and by six months of age a bloodhound puppy intended for work should be well versed in the art of hunting for its owner.

It is important to be able to control your hound, and whilst I don't 'obedience train' my hounds they should come when called, walk on a leash and be generally biddable.

I do not teach my hounds to track, but aim to get them to *hunt accurately*, always starting with a white flag and an article at the beginning of a line with a second flag after about twenty paces. This gets the hound used to what it will find at trials. After the first few preliminary 'infant lines' a harness is put on immediately prior to commencing work, so that the hound associates the harness, the flags and the article with hunting. As bloodhounds enjoy hunting, this aims to get them in the right frame of mind to track.

It is extremely important, in fact essential, that the handler knows *exactly* where the runner has gone. This is the fundamental basis of training a bloodhound, or any other breed, to track. You must know to the nearest foot where your runner has walked, exactly where the fence was crossed, or which end of the gate was used, etc., because only then can you put your hound right should it waver from the correct line. You must never correct your hound wrongly. A hunting hound is usually right unless you know better and to know better you must have knowledge of where the correct line is.

All bloodhounds can hunt people, sheep, rabbits etc., but you must teach your hound to hunt *only* people, and only one person, namely the runner, at a time, and it is this freedom from change of both species and individual which makes for the true and ideal tracking bloodhound.

To start with, puppies should be hunted in a tracking harness attached to a line or leash (thin nylon is light and usually adequate) and I prefer a really long cord (about 20 yd [18 m]) so that the hound gets used to working away from you and so that you do not get on top of your hound, and not only walk over the track but also contaminate it with your stronger scent. A long cord gives a hound more room to cast, which bloodhounds do naturally.

In the initial stages of instructing the puppy, everything should be made as easy as possible. The line should be very fresh, about fifteen minutes cold, and it should be short, and at the end when the puppy comes up to the runner, whom it probably knows at this stage, it should be encouraged to jump up. If you enter bloodhound trials there is nothing more depressing than for your hound to have completed a long and difficult line and then for it to fail to identify the runner at the end, to the satisfaction of the judge. Therefore, start young and encourage your hound always to identify the runner and if you teach it to jump up, whilst not being essential, it does ensure that the judge can see without difficulty that your hound knows who it has been hunting.

When your hound is competent on fifteen minute lines you can progress to half hour cold lines. This is quite cold enough at this stage as everything must be made as easy and pleasant as possible and it is a mistake to make lines difficult too early. Put in twists and turns on the tracks and often electric or telephone wires can be used to walk under, because the handler knows exactly where the track goes and the hound will not realise that it is following directly under an overhead wire. The handler must always know where the line goes.

A hound which only hunts on land with bracken and heather will find conditions very different on grassland or plough and training on all types of ground is important. Crossing roads, hunting along road edges and actually on tarmac and concrete are all part of later training.

A bloodhound must be safe with all types of stock and every opportunity should be taken to give puppies access to sheep, lambs, chickens, cats etc. while they are young and so more easily brought under control in the event of a chase.

It is a curious thing, but hounds that are perfectly used to sheep normally, when meeting the blackfaced sheep often found on moorland will occasionally give chase. One needs to be most cautious at all times when these sheep are about, as they seem to have some special attraction scentwise.

As judges are usually mounted at bloodhound trials, hounds should be used to horses and, if possible, worked with a horse near or behind them so that it is not an extra hazard when they enter the trials. The sound of galloping hooves can be quite unnerving to a young hound not used to such a thing.

If you have a good hound it will probably be far faster than its handler when hunting and it should always be encouraged to hunt on, not waiting for some tired handler to catch up. It must therefore learn to jump fences and other obstacles. You cannot expect to win at trials if the hound is waiting for you to catch up with it at every gateway for it to be let through. It must be encouraged to find a way over, round or through obstacles when on its training lines and the runner must walk to ensure that the hound has to find a way round, so that it becomes second nature to it. Fit not fat, should be the motto for a working hound. Even if the handler is a physical wreck, the hound should be fit and I'm sure that roadwork either beside a bicycle, behind a car or with a horse is one of the best ways of keeping a hound in shape. There is no doubt that nosework takes a lot out of even the fittest hound and your chances of success are marred if your entry is unfit.

Once you have taught your hound to hunt man in the proper manner and it knows the basics, then it is time to let it work off the leash. A bloodhound works much better when it is free to cast where it wishes, unmolested by cord. As lines become colder in competition so hounds, as you would expect, have to work more carefully and so progress more slowly, making it easier for the handler to keep up and keep control of the hound when hunting loose.

In ordinary working trials (as opposed to bloodhound working trials) dogs are tracked on a leash. Years ago it was usual for the handler to run after his dog, with the result that a fit tracking dog with an exhausted and often collapsed handler won the day, as time was then of the essence. Fortunately, when police work with dogs came on the scene, it was realised that such a handler would be quite incapable of apprehending a criminal in such circumstances, and now at these trials the dog is encouraged to pull the handler, i.e. keeping a tight leash, who walks behind his dog at a smart walking pace, and speed is not the most important feature. Bloodhound trials have evolved through the hunting field and as the judge is mounted and enjoys a good gallop, bloodhounds are encouraged to hunt at speed, as the only arrest that can be anticipated is that of cardiac arrest of the handler struggling to keep up. It may be that in years to come bloodhound trials may alter for the benefit of the handlers if not of the hounds.

Once your bloodhound has obtained its Working Permit, it is first entered in the Novice Stake, but you must not be disappointed if your hound, which hunts beautifully and successfully at home, does not put up its best performance at its first trials. Everything will be new to both hound and handler: the ground, the people, their cars, the horses and the noise of other bloodhounds. Once your hound gets used to this, it will soon come to know when it is going to trials and what they are all about.

The Novice Stake is often the most difficult stake to get out of, as to progress to Junior Stake your hound must either win Novice or come 2nd, and competition is keen; entries are usually large by comparison with other stakes, and the winning line usually both accurate and fast.

However, as the stakes become more advanced it is important to practise cross-tracks when hunting your hound in practice. You need a third person to walk directly across the line your hound is about to hunt, perhaps with a dog and crossing several times. You must know *exactly* where the cross is, so that you are in a position to correct the hound if it makes any attempt to change lines. It is always easier for a hound to hunt a fresher scent than the one it is meant to be hunting, but it is also more difficult for it to distinguish between two scents which are laid down at the same time. The object, therefore, is to teach it not to change to a different scent from the one on the article which it was given at the start of the track. The cross-track at first should be put down about fifteen minutes after the true line has been walked, later on, when your hound is reliable, the cross-track should be laid at the same time, and both lines should eventually continue together for part of the way. When your hound can be relied upon over cross-tracks then it is only a question of time before you win all the stakes.

As lines get colder they become more difficult for the hound and in my view it is not a good idea to persist training on very cold lines. A quick hunt on a half hour cold line for an experienced hound will give it enjoyment and still keep it on its toes. However, one must practise cold lines and again you must know exactly where the line goes, for some hounds as they get older tend to become 'dwellers' and will spend an inordinate amount of time going over the same bit of track. If you are to stop this, then you must push them on, otherwise it becomes a bad habit, and to do that you must know the line *exactly*. Of course if you only hunt your hounds four times a year at trials you cannot expect the best results.

Many judges like to see competitors encouraging their hounds as is often done in the hunting field to the extent of using hunting horns, and hunting whoops and noises. My view is that it is fine to encourage a hound when it is correct on its line, and at the start between the flags it is the obvious place to do this. Similarly on training lines you can encourage your hound because you know exactly when it is right, but to encourage it when it is wrong is thoroughly bad practice. Therefore, as the handler will not know when the hound is exactly right at a working trials (except by reading the hound), all forms of unnecessary encouragement should be curtailed once your hound can hunt properly. That does not mean that it should not be encouraged at the right time, and by experience a handler soon comes to know when that is, but it does mean that indiscriminate and unnecessary noise is not on and it can surely only distract a hound which is endeavouring to sort out a difficult scenting problem.

It is easy to tell when some hounds are tracking correctly but with others it may well be difficult. This is what is meant by reading your hound. Only by working your hound can you learn when to tell from looking at it whether it is on the line and hunting, whether it is casting about to find the line, or whether it has changed to something else. This is where experience comes in and it can only be learnt from watching your hound hunting and learning to interpret what it is doing in relation to the track. One thing is certain – if your hound is hunting quietly and suddenly starts to speak and hunt fast and furiously then you can be sure it has changed lines and is after a hare or deer or something similar and must be corrected.

If two hounds are hunted together they will usually speak and a speaking hound should be encouraged. However, many hounds will not speak when working alone. If your hound does not speak it is worth finding someone with a speaking hound so that it can learn the art and so hopefully continue speaking to the correct line when it again hunts alone. There are cups offered for the best speaking hounds. Whatever happens you do not want a babbler, which bays all the time whether hunting correctly or not.

Books, articles and much discussion centres around the subject of scent and what makes good and bad scenting conditions. Even the experts agree that the subject is not fully understood. However, it is very unwise to try to train a young hound in bad scenting conditions. Forgetting all the complicated theories of scent, if one remembers the one fact that 'hot air rises', then you can have some idea of what scenting conditions to expect. For example, on a cold day the ground is warmer than the cold air and therefore heat will rise and scent should be all right. On a hot summer day the ground will be hot but the air will be hotter and so you would not expect there to be much scent. In fact, tracking in hot weather is best confined to the early morning or late evening when there is dew on the ground.

In conclusion, remember that hunting the bloodhound is a sport and competitors at trials should always show a true sporting spirit. There can often be imperfections both in the management and judging at trials but providing you keep up training with your hound then undoubtedly your turn will come to take the prizes.

Miss Leonarda Pogodzinski

Miss Pogodzinski is the current Working Trials Secretary of the Association of Bloodhound Breeders; she is also an experienced trialer, and has worked with the Peak Bloodhound pack.

My desire to own a bloodhound began in 1964. I have always been fond of scent hounds and have always loved the countryside and hunting, so it was natural that I should want to own a hound that I could hunt myself. I also saw a picture of Barset of Barchester, whom I thought was a magnificent looking animal, and that made up my mind for me – what I wanted was a bloodhound.

First, I had to find someone who dealt in hounds which were solely used for hunting and which had the conformation to be able to go across country. I was recommended to contact the Furness family who kept the famous Peak Bloodhounds. Eric Furness, the Master, Huntsman and owner of the Peak Bloodhound pack, made arrangements for me to go and see his hounds and puppies.

When at a later date I purchased a bloodhound puppy, the Furnesses helped me to hunt the hound and introduced me to the Association of Bloodhound Breeders. Consequently, my hound and I went to working trials, where my hound showed the natural ability to hunt well, but was severely hampered by his not so knowledgeable handler. I can remember several Novice Stakes where judges thought how well my hound could hunt and how he was handicapped by me. Nevertheless, over a short period of time we improved: I learnt a great deal from my first bloodhound.

After my visits to the Furness establishment and a steady progress with my hound, Eric offered me a job looking after the Peak Bloodhounds and the horses. I accepted this and have never regretted going there. The Peak Bloodhounds were a very even pack, a super black and tan, had excellent bone and feet, and just the right amount of wrinkle: to be able to go across country at the speed they went it was necessary for the hounds to be able to see to enable them to negotiate fences etc. safely.

With bloodhounds the risk of bloat is always present. I believe hounds should always be exercised before feeding and rested for a while after exercise. I also think they should be walked out in the evening and looked at last thing at night before one retires for the day. I personally believe that a rigid routine – a regular diet given at the same time every day and regular exercise – can reduce the risk of bloat.

To be successful in owning a pack of bloodhounds one has to be more than dedicated. I don't think that bloodhounds are really suitable as pack hounds. They are very hard to manage because they are very much individuals right from the puppy stage. They are not quarrelsome amongst themselves and don't care for being severely rated. They also don't like to be lifted when hunting and indeed are difficult to lift.

One of the aspects that is good about hunting a pack of bloodhounds is the voice. So often an individual hound will hunt mute. Both my own hounds give tongue when hunting, but not as much as I would like. Yet, both hounds are from Peak Bloodhound breeding. My oldest hound, Rector, who is now ten years old is an original Peak Bloodhound and spent the first two years of his life in the pack. Although he has done very well at field trials, I feel that he prefers to hunt in the presence of other hounds, and he also speaks more freely when with other hounds. He is a very wide casting hound and I find him, as an individual, difficult to read, yet his scenting powers are tremendous. I've known him wind his quarry a mile away and cut across country to identify his quarry. I feel many judges in bloodhounds today fail to accept these qualities in a bloodhound. They seem to prefer a hound that hunts footstep by footstep. Hounds that hunt with their head in the air seem to get overlooked. I personally feel that there are not many people qualified to judge bloodhounds these days. To judge them as foxhounds, I feel, is wrong.

My other hound, Rochester, is quite different to his father, Rector. His work is far more closely done and he is far easier to read and will work with you as a team. Rochester is not as independent as Rector, although his scenting powers are just as great, his speed across country is fast when the going is good, he can see clearly and takes his fences with ease and this is how I like a bloodhound to be. Rochester, to me, is every bit as good as his ancestors who were in the Peak pack. [Rochester is now a Working Trial Champion.]

It is also good to see the number of good hounds coming from the top show kennels, who find themselves in the hands of individuals who are keen to hunt. These hounds look remarkably different to some of their litter brothers and sisters who spend their time in the show ring. The hounds that work must be managed differently and they look very workman-like when they come out to trials, although some of them seem to have restricted vision due to too much wrinkle and therefore tend to be lacking in confidence. Unfortunately there are hounds who do bump into things when out hunting and even have to be helped over fences, and lifting a bloodhound over a fence is no joke. I can well remember an incident that happened when I was with the Peak Bloodhounds: while we were out on morning exercise one day, taking out the young entry for the following season, a certain hound which, for some unknown reason, used to get footsore, decided she wasn't going any further. Consequently I had to get off my horse, lift the hound in question and lay her across the front of the saddle. There she remained until we got back to kennels, quite happy to flop about on the horse, who didn't mind either. Eventually that hound's feet did harden to regular exercise, but she never wandered far from my horse.

We had several memorable incidents with the bloodhounds. Monday nights when they were bellringing at the village church, the whole pack would sing along with the bells. They would do the same on a Sunday morning and even when a wedding took place. One of the best hounds in the pack, Van Dyke, even used to sneak off whilst being walked out in the afternoons, and one would find him either across at the church or visiting someone in the village.

The great thing about hunting the clean boot is that you can arrange where you want the hound to go. In these days of modern, intensive farming, this is an advantage over other forms of hunting. Stock and crops are so highly valued that farmers prefer hounds to go round stock and not to go plundering across newly sown seeds and winter corn.

As far as the choice between hunting a pack of hounds and hunting an individual hound is concerned, I would think it is a personal decision. Having done both and I would say that one can get as much fun out of hunting a single hound or a couple of hounds as one can get from hunting a pack. However, having been spoilt by the Peak Bloodhounds I would more than likely find myself being highly critical of other packs should they not be of the same standard as the Peak.

Bloodhounds even enable the worker in a town or city to do his own hunting, with the Association of Bloodhound Breeders and the Bloodhound Club organising field trials and weekend training events. The various enthusiasts even have their own hunting nuclei all over the country. Farmers and landowners seem to be most helpful in allowing us to go across their land. I am sure bloodhounds will play an important part in the hunting of the future.

Lady Rosemary Brudenell Bruce

Lady Rosemary still hunts her hounds, and her father, The Earl of Cardigan (later 6th Marquess of Ailesbury), was a founder of the Association of Bloodhound Breeders and for many years its President.

In this country, bloodhounds have been largely used for sport and police work. Their natural inclination for running a human scent, their persistence and ability to overcome every obstacle made them the dread of miscreants.

It is the object of bloodhound trials to foster these unique tendencies, and they have been the means of developing a highly exacting sport which is today the hobby of so many who love hounds, but could never otherwise hope to experience the joys and problems of being a huntsman. Hunting the clean boot exhibits the great perseverance and amazing ability of the trained hound to distinguish the individual scent it is required to follow, and to identify at the end of the hunt the person whose scent it had been given. I believe the law still accepts as conclusive evidence the identification of a bloodhound. The great importance of identification is too often overlooked.

I well remember at a bloodhound trial a good performance being sadly halted in the last field by a tractor and roller obliterating the

The Earl of Cardigan (later 6th Marquess of Ailesbury) with his bloodhounds at Tottenham Stables.

scent. In the distance some twenty people hopefully awaited the finish of the line. Sadly, I caught up my hound and proceeded to the far side of the field, where on the headland I loosed the hound, and we walked slowly past the spectators. Suddenly down went the bitch's head as the scent was regained and she plunged into the crowd to identify her runner. A disappointing end had become a joyful triumph to both hound and handler and a pleasure to the runner and spectators.

And what of packs of bloodhounds? In otherwise hopeless environments, and in an atmosphere of growing reluctance to the hunting of wild animals, are they not the obvious answer?

Undoubtedly the hunting of a human quarry has much to recommend it, in the avoidance of dangerous roads, private property, and the many hazards that make hunting a pack of fox or deerhounds impracticable. However, the bloodhound is not a natural pack hound. Only years of selective breeding and much drafting can hope to produce a pack that will run together against their natural individualism.

Where the hunt must consider the desire of their followers to gallop and jump, draghounds, or if these are regarded as too artificial, part-bred bloodhound-foxhounds, are in my opinion the best choice.

Most pure-bred packs of bloodhounds are privately owned, and the ability of the huntsman, backed up by an active and understanding whipper-in, will determine the success or otherwise of their performance in the hunting field. Nothing is more odious than arriving at the finish of a hunt with a few leading hounds, leaving the rest of the pack scattered disheartedly in the rear.

With voice and horn every hound must be encouraged to reach the end triumphantly. As Sir Henry Bentinck so rightly wrote in his classic *Foxhounds and Their Handling in the Field*, 'It is impossible to over-estimate the mischief done to a pack of hounds by unfairly and habitually leaving a hound behind, out of its place. It is teaching them to be rogues.' How true!

To all this must be added the distressing possibility of losing the runner, with the knowledge that you cannot draw for another. And the still more embarrassing situation of hounds changing from the runner to some unsuspecting members of the public who fail to appreciate being the quarry.

Perhaps a pack of bloodhounds may not after all be the huntsman's dream.

Eric Furness M.H., Master of the Peak Bloodhounds

Having hunted bloodhounds for about forty years, it may be that a few comments may be of interest.

Breeding and hunting a small pack of some five or six couple of hounds was always my main interest. Before World War 2 I hunted a few couple on foot one day a week throughout the winter, and great sport was had. I might say that one needs to be young and fit to hunt a pack of bloodhounds on foot. The advent of war put an end to this venture but when the war was over I restarted a mounted pack. I hunted only the 'clean boot', and we met twice a week from October to May. My little pack of some half a dozen couple of hounds was entirely private and mounted followers were by invitation only.

As a rule two or three lines were hunted each day, each line being 6–12 miles [10–20 km] in length and one or two hours cold, the coldness of the line being varied according to the scenting conditions and the length of the line. I was very fortunate to live in grass and stone wall country where scenting conditions were usually fairly good. The local packs of foxhounds and harriers in whose country I hunted were always most helpful. It is absolutely essential to establish good relations with any pack which hunts in the area, and ensure that nothing is done to interfere with their sport.

The best hunt I ever had was in the Peak District of Derbyshire when I hunted a line two hours cold and 13 miles [21 km] in length in 65 minutes, and every hound up at the end.

My hounds were kennelled as a pack of foxhounds and had two hours' mounted road exercise daily during the season. I always kept 10 or 12 couple of hounds and on occasions hunted the full pack, but the best days were always with a small pack.

In the first place one should realise that the bloodhound is not a natural pack hound, being much too independent by nature, and in my opinion is not suitable to be hunted in a large pack followed by a hard riding field whose main ambition is to jump as many fences as possible. However, first class sport may be had with a small well matched pack, and I think that the ideal situation is some five or six couple of hounds followed by the huntsman, whipper-in and three or four dedicated people who really appreciate hound work. A bloodhound must have room to make his cast, and if given space will cast back to where he last held the line, whereas the foxhound tends to drive forward. Bloodhounds certainly lack drive and if they are overridden they quickly lose interest and become sulky.

It is a very difficult and long process to breed a pack of bloodhounds, as opposed to an heterogenous collection of hounds. I regret to say that the latter state of affairs is seen all too often. Due to their very individual style of hunting they must be well matched as regards speed, otherwise they will string out instead of carrying a good head.

Voice is of paramount importance, a mute hound is an abomination and should be drafted at once. I am afraid that bloodhounds have lost a lot of voice in recent years, and although

Reg R. Wright M.H. (*left*) and Eric Furness M.H. (*right*) at working trials.

the reason for this is not apparent, there is no doubt that tongue is hereditary and when once lost is very difficult to bring back. I really do implore breeders to give this problem their most urgent attention, as there is no hound with such a magnificent voice as a bloodhound. Remember the words of Whyte-Melville in his poem of the Ranston Bloodhounds, 'How the chorus pealed and gathered to an organs tone'. It is a well known fact that bloodhounds are much more free with their tongue when hunting an animal as quarry as opposed to the 'clean boot'. I remember years ago that there was a certain hound at the trials who only spoke when he was rioting. What a ghastly animal.

Unfortunately bloodhounds are cursed with a very delicate constitution. Probably the most serious problem is bloat, which accounts for the death of many hounds each year, and little progress has been made regarding prevention or cure during my lifetime. Entropion is another common affliction, and I think that I am safe in saying that this is a legacy of exaggerated breeding by show people who seem intent on producing a canine tadpole. Let me hasten to add that all individuals who are only interested in working their hounds should be mindful of the fact that without the exhibitors the bloodhound would have become extinct during the last two wars. Having said this I must also point out that I am not grateful to anyone whose desire is to produce an animal with such an abundance of wrinkle that the poor creature is prevented from seeing where he is going when his nose is on the ground. If only breeders would concentrate on breeding hounds of quality, free from exaggeration I am certain that it would be ultimately a great benefit to the breed. I hope that I have not given the impression

Eric Furness M.H. with the Peak Bloodhounds on Stannale Moor, Derbyshire.

that I have a poor opinion of all show hounds; this is not the case, and I am the first to admit that there are a number of hounds being shown today that would be perfectly capable of doing an honest day's work.

To return to the question of constitution, it seems that the weaknesses which hounds suffer from in these days were not always present. The Count Le Couteulx de Canteleu in his book *Manuel de Venerie Française* which was published in 1890, praises the constitution of the bloodhound, and his great ability to withstand extremes of temperature. However, Edwin Brough writing in 1906 is very worried about the inherent weaknesses of the breed, and is of the opinion that an outcross is essential from time to time. I quote, 'If there are still sticklers for what they unthinkingly call purity of blood let them consider, after reading the following particulars of out-crosses made within the writers recollection, what a comparative term this purity is.' He then goes on to give a long list of all the outcrosses used around the turn of the century.

As I consider this question of constitution of such paramount importance, I will quote further: 'A little later came the blind worship of pedigree, which for the average breeder, consisted of a string of meaningless names representing animals quite unknown to him. His only idea was to bow down to the fetish "thoroughbred" not realising that a pedigree composed entirely of thoroughbred wasters might be vastly inferior to one consisting chiefly of animals representing the best of their breed, which had continuously reproduced the required qualities for many generations, although it is possible to breed out any faults by outcrossing within the breed, but unfortunately in the case of the bloodhound this is not so, since all the animals are closely related, due to the comparative scarcity of hounds. Importation of hounds from abroad does not solve the problem since they are all bred from exports from this country, and suffer from the same defects, hence the new blood must of necessity come from a different breed.'

I feel that at this juncture I should warn people that outcrossing is a very dangerous exercise unless it is undertaken by a skilful and experienced breeder. After World War 2, when the bloodhound was at a very low ebb, an outcross was used with great success. The majority of the top trial hounds carried this blood, the first Working Trial Champions after the war, WT Ch. Raycroft Jailer and WT Ch. Raycroft Jasmine, were both full of this blood, as were many of the hounds winning on the bench. In my opinion the Kennel Club have shown an astonishing lack of wisdom in virtually closing the door on the introduction of a further outcross. The outcross used in this case was that of a hound from the kennels of the Dumfriesshire foxhounds, by the generosity of the late Sir John Buchanan-Jardine, who together with his son, Sir Rupert Buchanan-Jardine, are acknowledged as two of the greatest hound breeders of this century.

During the late 1960s I found that my pack was losing constitution, and after much thought and advice from Sir Rupert Buchanan-Jardine I decided to use a black and tan Dumfriesshire foxhound bitch. This bitch was by a Gascon-Saintongeois which Sir Rupert had imported from France, and as these French hounds have excellent nose and voice, it was hoped that the offspring would retain these most desirable qualities. This proved to be the case, and the first cross hunted the 'clean boot' almost as well as the pure bloodhound, although it must be admitted that they were not quite as staunch. However, when these hounds were put back to the pure bloodhound, this defect was quickly rectified, and the second cross hounds were almost indistinguishable from the pure bloodhound as regards type and work, but, most important of all, had robust constitutions.

Alas, an old spinal injury forced me to give up riding, and the hounds were disbanded. Some of them continued to hunt the 'clean boot' in other packs, and others went to France to hunt roe deer where they were a great success and 'nicked' well with the French hounds.

If these few comments have given food for thought, I shall be more than satisfied.

6
Bloodhounds for Police and Army Work

Today's law enforcement methods have, from necessity, changed considerably from those of the last century. The speed and efficiency with which modern lawbreakers act, have forced the development of new detection methods. One of the changes that has occurred has affected the type of dog used. No longer are the scenting powers considered to be of paramount importance; today's police or army dogs must show versatility and obedience above all else. These requirements are fulfilled by breeds such as the German shepherd dog and the Labrador. However, I believe that when it comes to finding a lost child or pursuing a criminal over hard, trackless land, the bloodhound remains supreme and I do wish that for these purposes, more use was made and encouraged of him.

Cuttings from the Kennel Club Brough Records

In order to put the discussion of the role of bloodhounds in modern police and army work in perspective, I include here a selection of items from the Kennel Club Brough records, which give a colourful and interesting picture of the use of bloodhounds in England during the second half of the last century.

Kennel Gazette, December 1860.
    A little girl of 12 years of age was missed from her home in Leeds last month and the police having reason to believe that she'd been murdered, searched a wood near with bloodhounds without, we

believe, any clue being obtained. We've often wondered why bloodhounds are not made more practical use of than they are, to assist in tracing and detecting crime as we can point to more than one murder that has been found out, mainly by their instrumentality within the last few years. There was a fearful murder of a girl only a year or so ago and in all human probability would never have been detected if it had not been for the sagacity and delicate nose of nearly pure bred bloodhound.

To the Editor of the *Kennel Gazette*, January 1881.

Sir, I was very glad to see in the December number of the Kennel Gazette, a suggestion that bloodhounds should be systematically kept and used by the police. Mr. Ray mooted this question for sometime since, but unfortunately it was allowed to drop through. I would beg all bloodhound breeders to train some of their hounds for manhunting....

I would also suggest to the Committee of the Kennel Club that the experiment of a bloodhound trial be made at the summer Kennel Club show. If it were very dry weather it would have to be run early in the morning. Care should be taken that the man should not be known to any of the hounds entered and that nothing is rubbed on his shoes. Keepers should not be allowed to lift or assist their hounds in any way. The hounds would be strange to each other and jealousy should probably carry them over the scent, but they should be able to cast themselves and recover the line.

I believe that bloodhound trials would be popular and cannot conceive any better method of drawing attention to the capabilities of the breed. About a year ago I received a letter one Sunday from a gentleman in Wales asking me to send a man with a couple of bloodhounds to assist in a murder case. I did not send the hounds as they could not have reached their destination before Monday afternoon and I thought it little or no use. I found afterwards that the murder had been committed on the Wednesday, on a public highway where people were constantly passing. If everyone had as high an opinion as this gentleman of the power of the bloodhound, he would soon be more frequently called into use. Hoping that you will encourage the expression of the opinions of other breeders on this matter.

I am, Sir, your obedient servant, Edwin Brough.
Leek. December 29th, 1880.

Opposite: Posed by WT Ch. Sanguine Saturn.

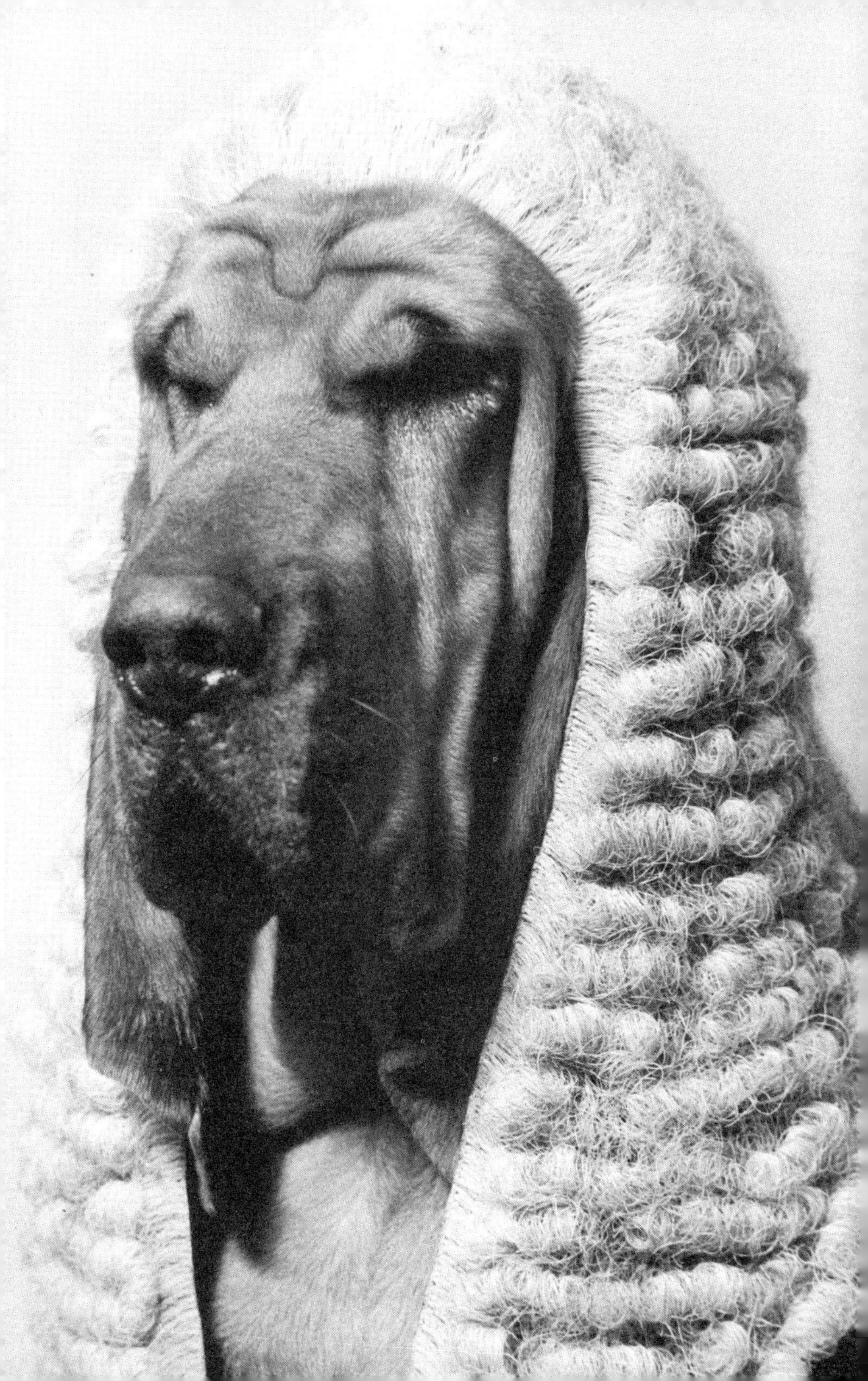

P.S. I know no reason why a couple of bloodhounds on any large manor should not be an almost certain preventative of poaching as they are held in great dread and in this case they should be used on a lead.

From the Editor: (We've already drawn attention to the practical use of bloodhounds might be made of in detecting crime. The following quaint advertisement appeared in an Irish paper a few days ago: 'Notice is hereby given that on and after the 1st of January, instant, a fierce mastiff dog in charge of a keeper will be enlarged in Blankpark every night at ten o'clock for the purpose of detecting and pursuing trespassers after game. All those having no legitimate business in the park after that hour are cautioned to beware'. 'Editor'.)

To the Editor of the *Kennel Gazette*, February 1881.

Sir, I shall feel obliged if you can find space for the following extract which I have met with since writing the letter you kindly inserted in last month's Gazette:

(From *Bewick's Quadrupeds*, published at Newcastle-on-Tyne, 1824).

'The Bloodhound'

The bloodhound was in great request with our ancestors as it was remarkable for the fineness of its scent. It was frequently employed in recovering game that had escaped, wounded from the hunters. It could follow with great certainty the footsteps of a man to a considerable distance and in barbarous and uncivilised times when a thief or murderer had fled, this useful creature would trace him from the thickest and most secret coverts, nor would it cease its pursuit till he had taken the felon.

For this reason there was a law in Scotland that who ever denied entrance to one of these dogs in the pursuit of stolen goods should be deemed an accessory. Bloodhounds were formerly used in certain districts lying between England and Scotland which were much infested by robbers and murderers and a tax was laid upon the inhabitants for keeping and maintaining a certain number of them. But as the arm of justice is now extended to every part of the country and there are no secret recesses where villainy can lie concealed, these services are no longer necessary. In Scotland it was distinguished by the name of 'Sleuth Hound'. Some few of these dogs are still kept in the southern part of the Kingdom and used in pursuit of deer that have been previously wounded by a shot to draw blood, the scent of which enables them to pursue with most unerring steadiness. They are sometimes used in discovering deer-stealers whom they infallibly trace by the blood of their victim. They are also said to be kept in convents situated in the lonely and mountainous countries of Switzerland, both as a guard to the sacred mansion, as well as to find out the bodies of men who may have been unfortunately lost in crossing those wild and dreary tracts.

The first public bloodhound trials were held in 1886 at Warwick Dog Show. The announcement of this event prompted the publication of a considerable number of letters and articles in the national press.

To the Editor of *The Field*, March 6th, 1886.
Utility of Bloodhounds in Chasing Criminals.
Sir, Seeing a reference made in the House of Commons on 26th Ult., to an advertisement in your paper, on the matter of bloodhounds, I write to put on record a case which once came under my notice showing the value of those animals for tracing a thief and bringing him to punishment. About the year 1834–1836 my father was living in a large and lonely house in the country and had a bloodhound given him whom we called Thunder. One morning his head farming man came in and said that during the night someone had killed one of the sheep and taken the carcase away, leaving the skin in a ditch. My father immediately went to Harlington, the nearest village for the constable, whom he found in the person of an old man and very shaky.

'I've had a sheep stolen and I want you to come and take up the thief,' said my father.

'Oh, I can't find him, Sir,' said the constable.

'I've a dog that will find him for you,' said my father.

'Oh, but I could not take him, Sir,' said the constable.

'Then you'd better take me and get me sworn in and I will help you to take him.'

My father being sworn in, the dog was taken on a chain to where the skin was, from which place Thunder pulled hard across two fields to a cottage door, on knocking on which a man appeared.

'I'm come for my sheep,' said my father.
'I've not got any sheep of yours,' said the man.
'Well, my dog says you have,' said my father.

The door being forced open, Thunder went straight to a heap of coals and began to scrape and soon expose the sheep. The man was transported. The dog was very good tempered and we boys used to pull his ears in order to make him bay at stated times to be heard by friends who lived a mile and a half off. Surely such dogs ought to be more used to trace murderers and such.

To the Editor of *The Field*, March 13th, 1886.
Utility of Bloodhounds in Chasing Criminals.
Sir, I am pleased to see this subject ventilated in your columns and hope that it may lead to the grandest hound being put to some practical use instead of being only a show dog and pet. That they can be used to hunt man without danger, I can give a case as proof, when Mr Nevill of Chilland first had his hounds from the New Forest now more than forty years ago – a man servant looking out of his window one moonlit night, saw a tramp take a turkey from a number roosting on some rails in front of the house, he put it under his arm and made off with it. He immediately dressed and called his master who also put on his clothes and then let out of the kennel a hound called 'Random' who immediately took up the line of the tramp. He must have been gone over half an hour, if not more than that as Mr Nevill was a cripple who could neither dress nor move about very quickly. Random ran him across some pastureland, throwing his tongue at intervals into the Winchester Road, where, however, he still held the line and it was a considerable distance until they came up to the turkey in the middle of the road, which the man finding he was pursued, dropped. Not really wishing to catch the man, as he had not made off with the bird, Mr Nevill stopped Random with very little trouble and took him home. This proving that he was quite enough under command to obviate any fear of his doing mischief.

Samuel Maynard, who was bred in the New Forest and afterwards went to Windsor whence he entered the service of the late Mr Fenwick Bisset as keeper and labourer, told me his family had been on a walk in the forest since the time of Queen Anne, if not longer and had for that period always had some of these hounds at their lodge. I think he said each keeper was bound to keep a couple of them in those days. One celebrated dog, called 'Hawser', he told me, was put on the line of a wounded buck and ran right away from his (Maynard's) father and the other keepers. But somehow, hours afterwards, brought the buck back to near where he was found, set him up to bay and Maynard shot him by moonlight. They found from other keepers afterwards, that he was heard running the buck at least 12 miles from where they started. At that time, there were thousands of fallow deer in the forest, but he hunted them without change. Maynard is, I believe, now living near Dunster and would no doubt tell more particulars about Hawser.

The Random mentioned was a very large dog and could reach anything he wanted from an ordinary dining room table if near the edge without removing his forefeet from the ground. I am nearly sure his back could not have gone under the table, but will not quite trust my memory on that point.

I sincerely trust that the bloodhound trials of Warwick may prove a success.

signed by H.H.

P.S. An old keeper of Mr Lowndes in Whatton Chase, who lives near me, has no end of anecdotes in catching sheep and deer stealers with bloodhound.

Bloodhounds in America

The introduction of two of Edwin Brough's hounds to America in 1888 inspired the following enthusiastic letter to the *American Field*.

To the Editor of the *American Field*, May 12th, 1888.
A Manhunt with English Bloodhounds.
Editor, *American Field*: By special request of Mr J. L. Winchell, the well known dog fancier, of this place, I visited his kennels and afterwards enjoyed the novel, but exciting sport of a manhunt. Some hours previous to my visit a man had been started away with instructions to choose the most difficult way he could find and to keep going until the hounds came up with him. After being courteously shown about the kennels and having seen many fine specimens of mastiffs and Great Danes, I was introduced, so to

speak, to the only two fully grown dogs of the kind in America, Matchley Venus and Berniston, both finely bred and trained English Bloodhounds from a Mr Brough in England. The term bloodhound had always been associated with something terrible in my mind and it was with much trepidation, I entered that commodious and well kept quarters. However what fear was felt was soon dispelled by the faithful and gentle disposition displayed by the animals. In form and general appearance Venus greatly resembled the deerhound of the Adirondacks though different in colour.

Berniston is a noble animal taller than Venus with intelligent and gentle eye. The ears however were quite ten inches long and the lips long and drooping with very little the look of a maneater about them. The old time ferocity of the breed having been washed out by careful breeding and training through many generations until now they possess all the old time instincts and sagacity and are as gentle and trusting as Spaniels.

Venus and Berniston were leashed and with Mr Winchell following one and I following the other, the hunt began, their noses closely trailing the ground, the hound at once starting on the track of the fugitive. It was an extremely warm afternoon and the hounds being eager for the hunt, it was only a very short time before a full dress suit of a Fiji Islander was greatly desired by one of the party at least. After proceeding about a quarter of a mile, the trail struck off through the fields leading over fences and finally into deep woods and frequently through swampy places. Here the wonderful instinct of these animals was best displayed. Most of the water was quite deep for some distance, but the trail was followed as readily as though it was on dry ground.

When the extreme condition failed the hounds would run from place to place until they gained upon the scent – and then away they would go, baying deeply and resonantly. Every way had been tried to puzzle the hounds by the fugitive – he had crossed and recrossed his trail, climbed trees and even retraced his steps for a distance. But there was no such thing as throwing the pursuers off his track, every turn taken by him was followed by them until miles had been travelled and he was finally overtaken. Then there was a pretty scene. The hounds by every means possible to their limited intelligence, expressed their pleasure at finding the object of their search. They leapt upon him and whined for gladness.

They are used in England to a great extent in hunting for persons who may become lost, rather than for retrievers or violators of the law and though unerring when put upon the track of the latter and closely followed, they are too gentle to be used after a free chase after desperate characters.

These dogs were brought here by Mr Winchell from the bench show in New York last March where they were exhibited by Mr E. Brough of Wyndgate, Nr. Scarborough, England. This is their first introduction into America and Mr Winchell was most fortunate in securing Mr Brough's consent to bring them to the Green Mountain Kennels for a short time, as it will undoubtedly lead to their being extensively bred here. Already Mr Winchell is receiving enquiries from all parts in relation to them, principally from the Western and South Western frontiers where they are wanted for police duty. Since coming here, Venus has littered four puppies which were sired by Bradshaw, the most noted dog of this strain in the world. Bradshaw died recently and the puppies are probably the most valuable of their kind on either side of the water.

Beside from his readiness at any and all times to show visitors the attraction of his kennels, Mr Winchell will at anytime, when he has leisure, be glad to exhibit to visitors the hunting qualities of Venus and Berniston. I can assure any who are so fortunate to go on a manhunt with them that this is the keenest and most exhilarating pleasure.

Signed: G.M.

Jack the Ripper

In 1888, the East End of London was the scene of a series of gruesome murders by one of the most notorious murderers of all time – Jack the Ripper. The police hunted this vicious killer with no success, and there was a great deal of correspondence, preserved now in the Brough records, in the national press concerning the use of bloodhounds to track him down.

In the event, bloodhounds were brought in, and although they did not succeed in tracing Jack the Ripper, no murders were committed during the time the hounds were housed in London. However, as soon as they were returned to their owners, the murders continued. Jack the Ripper was never caught.

Topical comment from a contemporary newspaper of 1888 dealing with the Whitechapel murders.

The St. James Gazette, October 2nd, 1888.
The East End Murders.
   Our detectives ought to go about their work with much more pliability and inventiveness. They cannot afford to neglect expedients which do not fall in with official traditions. Bloodhounds at a Metropolitan Police station may seem a trifle incongruous, but it is not so long ago that a murderer in England was tracked down by one of these animals; and if a trained bloodhound and somebody who understands him are available they should be got without delay. Nor need Scotland Yard be afraid to ask for outside aid.

Pall Mall, October 3rd, 1888.

Bloodhounds as Detectives.

For centuries the bloodhound has been employed as a detective. In ancient days he was supposed to have been introduced by the Normans to trace deer stealers who broke their stringent forest laws. Wallace and Bruce were both hunted by these hounds and an old manuscript tells how Bruce was sought for by Edward the First: 'The King Edward with horse and hound him sought'.

Doctor Johannes Caius one of the earliest writers on dogs was saying that during his day these animals were used in tracking criminals and during the times of border raiders, they were employed to trace the bold Moss-Troopers that had swept down from over the Scottish border. In one of the ballads it is told how Richard Musgrave 'By wily turns and desperate bounds had baffled Piercy's best bloodhounds'.

Nearly a century ago the Thrapston Association for the prosecution of felons had a trained bloodhound especially to track sheep stealers. Youatt tells how that on one occasion in order to test the dog, a man was given an hour start, but it secured him in an hour and a half concealed in a tree nearly fifteen miles from home.

Another instance has been recorded was how that a Mr Lawrence who was well-known as a sportsman early in the present century, had to discharge a groom who out of revenge returned to the stables and mutilated a favourite hunter. He was traced by means of a bloodhound for twenty miles – the hound finding the fellow in bed, who seeing escape impossible confessed his crime.

Poachers have often been chased by bloodhounds as have fugitive slaves in America and Cuba. Several pages might be written and illustrated of the marvellous scenting powers at almost every variety of circumstance of the bloodhound.

One of the most recent cases was in Blackburn about twelve years ago when Fish, who had murdered a little girl, was convicted by a hound. The question at once arises as to how the service of a bloodhound can be secured as speedily as possible after a crime is discovered. In such a matter as this time is all important although we should not despair at following the trail some hours after it was made and been traversed by hundreds of other trails – yet the fresher it is, the more certain it is to succeed. It would be inadvisable for the police to keep the dogs themselves since as soon as the present scare has passed away, the animals would probably be neglected. But if a register of all bloodhounds could be made and an arrangement made with the owners so that they could be at the disposal of the police whenever required. A small subsidy would be money well spent. At the present time there are kennels of bloodhounds at the South Lambeth Road, in Kensington, Dulwich, Putney, Regents Park and we believe in the E.C. district. On Sunday morning any of these could have been procured in a couple of hours at the most and there is every probability that if such had been done, the culprit or culprits might have been safely in Newgate ere London had known one word of this, its latest

Contemporary cartoons relating to bloodhounds in the Jack the Ripper case.

horror. Surely the thing is worth a trial and we doubt not Mr Mark Beaufoy of Lambeth or Mr E. Nichols of Kensington or in fact any bloodhound owner would place these dogs at the disposal of the police authorities under proper conditions.

Steps should be taken at once in this direction. It would be of comparatively little use acting after the murder is committed – we mean the making of arrangements should not be left until then, for the owners of the dogs should be seen, and a list of those available hung in every police station with directions as to how they can most speedily be secured. If bloodhounds can be employed to hunt escaped slaves and law breaking criminals, surely there need be no compunction as to their use for brutal murderers.

To the Editor of *The Times*, October 8th, 1888.

Sirs, Since the bloodhound ceased to be used in the pursuit of sheep stealers, it has become scarce and is chiefly regarded as an ornament to our dog shows and a model for the artist. I hope that you will allow me a little space to advocate the restoration of this noble hound to his old position in the detection of crime.

I may say that I have been a breeder of bloodhounds for nearly twenty years and have had some experience in training to hunt 'The Clean Boot' and take great interest in the history of the breed and its great possibility of usefulness. I have found that most people have the impression that the bloodhound is a savage treacherous brute. I think this idea is a result of recollections of 'Uncle Tom's Cabin' and books of that kind. The Cuban bloodhound which was used for slave hunting was a savage animal and would pull his man down when he came up to him. This is quite a different breed from our bloodhound and does not resemble him at all in appearance or disposition. I often run men that my hounds have never seen and when the hounds come up and lick them all over, they take no further interest in them. The bloodhound may be of great use in tracking criminals but would be of little service in capturing them. In Moss Trooping times it was not uncommon thing to run a scent of a man that had ten or fifteen hours start and do so successfully – although the hounds of that time were so slow that when the pursuers came to soft ground and the track was plain they took up the hound and carried him on the saddles to save time and laid him on again when they came to hard ground. I have letters from two men that have charge of hounds

A. Sewell, veterinary surgeon, was asked by Sir Charles Warren to procure bloodhounds for the Ripper case. This letter, to Edwin Brough, is one of many that Mr Sewell wrote to bloodhound owners throughout Britain requesting the loan of some hounds.

that are attached to penitentiaries in Texas. They gave the most wonderful accounts of capture of convicts with hounds although the men in some instances had twenty four to thirty six hours start. In one case they ran their man over forty miles. These hounds are crossed between the Cuban bloodhound and Foxhounds and are splendidly trained and kept constantly at their work. Our English bloodhound is infinitely superior to this or to any other breed in natural scenting power while luckily our breeders have developed the long narrow peaked head and immense flews always associated with this faculty to an extent never known before. The misfortune is that most owners of bloodhounds never take the trouble to train them and although the latent power is there, all the hounds being very easily entered to manhunting, it will take some years of careful training to obtain the best results. If a few intelligent men who have had some experience in working hounds or in breaking dogs to the gun would take the matter up, the capability of the bloodhound would be made so manifest that he would be constantly used by the police and the deterrent effect would be incalculable. The bloodhound can hunt a lighter scent than any other hound and, when properly trained, will stick to the line of a hunted man, although it may have been crossed by others. I doubt whether there are any bloodhounds in England sufficiently trained to have a good chance of tracking a man in a crowded thoroughfare such as Whitechapel.

Unless laid on at once the chances are that the hound might hit off the wrong trail. But if a well trained bloodhound had been tried at Gateshead before the scene of the murder had been much trampled over he would have been very likely to run the man down.

Some years since a so-called bloodhound had caused great excitement in connection with a Blackburn murder. This animal was a mongrel with little or no trace of bloodhound about it but led to the discovery of the murderer by finding some bones concealed in the chimney.

Of course any other cur would have done as much. The great value of the pure bloodhound is that he can be trained to hunt the scent of a man through his boots without any artificial aid such as blood. It is scarcely likely that the murderer will be so obliging as to smear his boots with the blood of his victim. I shall be pleased to give any further information to anyone interested in the training of

Trial in Hyde Park, 1888, with Sir Charles Warren, to test Edwin Brough's bloodhounds, Barnaby and Burgho.

bloodhounds or to answer any enquiries that may suggest themselves to your readers.

Edwin Brough.
Wyndgate, near Scarborough. October 5th.

To the Editor of the *Evening News*, Tuesday, October 9th, 1888.
Bloodhounds in Hyde Park.
Sir, As I see from this morning's papers that official information has been supplied to the press upon the subject of the bloodhounds that have been brought to London to track the Whitechapel murderer, I shall presume I shall not be making any indiscrete disclosure by giving an account of the trial run that was made this morning in Hyde Park in the presence of the Commissioner of the Police. I will preface the description by a few remarks showing how bloodhounds were introduced in this matter.

It has long been the opinion among breeders and exhibitors of dogs that the keen scenting power of the bloodhound should be more generally employed in the detection of crime.

The chief objection to the proposal has been the one of a sentimental nature. An important number of the public abhore the idea of employing a means which calls up having thoughts of the days when escaped slaves were trapped by bloodthirsty dogs and the very name bloodhound possesses a terror for many minds.

These objectives may be dismissed in a couple of words as far as they effect the hounds Sir Charles Warren has summoned to London. In the first place, the dogs used for hunting slaves in America were not bloodhounds at all but a variety of crossbreeds – Mastiff type predominantly. Secondly, the title 'Bloodhound' is an unfortunate misnomer as applied to the animals we recognise nowadays by this name. For our bloodhound is a descendant from the French St Hubert hound as anybody can recognise who's seen the same breed in France, where it is still used for its natural purpose hunting in packs, deer and other quarry. I have already fully explained this in the columns of the *Stockkeeper and Fanciers' Chronicle* advocating calling the bloodhound by his old name 'The St Hubert' which is correct and not repellent.

How the Hounds were Procured
Last Thursday an eminent veterinary surgeon of the South West district was summoned by telegraph to attend Sir Charles Warren

to advise upon the question of employing bloodhound for the discovery of the Whitechapel murderer.

His views being favourable to the plan, he was instructed to procure hounds. He immediately communicated with two well known breeders who were known to have trained their hounds to hunt man. Mr Hood Wright offered his famous Hector II who so distinguished himself at the Warwick dog show trials that on condition that should any harm come to it he should be compensated to the extent of £100. Mr Edwin Brough replied that he would bring to town two thoroughly trained hounds, Barnaby and Burgho if his expenses were paid. The second offer was accepted. They arrived last Saturday in time for what was expected by the police would take place on Sunday night. They were kennelled by Mr W. K. Taunton. Yesterday, Monday 7 a.m. they were tried in Regents Park by the owner and the veterinary surgeon. They were out again last night and hunted on the leash in the dark.

The Meet in Hyde Park

On both these occasions their performance gave the greatest satisfaction and Sir Charles Warren when he received the report made an appointment to attend a trial himself this morning at Albert Gate. Hyde Park at 7 a.m. was chosen for the meet.

At a quarter to the hour I was the first on the ground. A few minutes later a gentleman, one of the chief surgeons to the police arrived. At 7, Mr Brough, Mr Taunton and a friend came in a trap with the two hounds. Six minutes later, Sir Charles Warren rode up on a stout cob directly after the veterinary surgeon arrived attended by his assistant.

No time was lost in making a start; the morning was fine, but misty and a slight wind blew from the east. It felt like a fine hunting morning, but it turned out to be the contrary again proving how difficult it is until the hounds are on, to say if scent will lie.

Sir Charles offers Himself as a Quarry

Sir Charles immediately offered to act as a hunted man. No scent of any shape was used. The hounds were to hunt nothing but the plain boot of a man they had no previous knowledge of.

The Chief Commissioner set off at a trot in the direction of

Brough lent two hounds, Barnaby and Burgho, to the police in October 1888. Unfortunately, they remained on the case for under a month, the authorities being unable to agree to the charges for insurance, keep, hire, etc.

Bayswater. After he had been given ample time and had passed out of sight, Mr Brough with a wave of his hat and an encouraging cheer slipped the intelligent couple of hounds who galloped off carrying their heads low with their long pendulous ears sweeping the morning dew from the grass. They did not bay at all but hunted perfectly mute.

 Sir Charles made a circle round and the hounds went at a fair pace, not fast – when he traversed about half the circle he called to a constable to cross his track which the man did. This point the hounds checked – they made a careful slow cast, Barnaby hitting it off, Burgho followed then they ran it closely until they winded their man some twenty yards from the track and then they were at fault and we came up to them. Sir Charles having plenty of wind left, decided to give us another run. Again the hounds were laid on but did not work so well and it became apparent to us that it was a very bad morning for scent.

Mr H. B. Shepard is Hunted

The Chief Commissioner agreed that another member of our party, Mr H. B. Shepard, who is well up in drag and showhound work should give us a run. Mr Shepard set off in a northerly direction. After he had gone some seven hundred yards, a baker's boy crossed and directly after, a man walked over the track. We then lost sight of our man in the mist. When we viewed him again emerging from Kensington way, we laid on. The hounds swept along pausing a moment where the track had been foiled by the footsteps of the boy and the man. About half the distance they were at fault and Burgho ran back, but Barnaby casting forward found and finished well. By this time the park was filling so we called up the hounds. In spite of the scent not allowing, Sir Charles Warren was able to see sufficient to recognise the value of the hounds for their purpose. They hunted perfect strangers and stuck to them when others crossed the scent. They had no scent but the odour of man and leather.

Ready for the Next Murder

These hounds will be kept where they can be summoned instantly and within reach of Whitehall in less than half an hour. Should another murder take place, the man who discovers the body must without a word to passers-by repair to the nearest police station whence the hounds will be wired for.

If this be done as I've described, the complications of track by many feet will be avoided and I have no doubt whatever that the murderer will be run down.

The Murderer Will Carry the Drag

Hounds that can hunt a boot with a bad injury scent, will never check after a man who in addition to his natural body odour animated by excitement will most probably get splashed by a little blood and then in addition to these advantages the man after having his hands in the abdomen will bear fresh and strong that sickly smell which surgeons know clings to the hands for days and after repeated washing with carbolic soap, and, further this murderer by removing and retaining one of the organs when he takes the uterus or kidney will be actually carrying the drag for the hounds. With such an accumulation of scent particles these bloodhounds will track hours after the man has got away and if within a 100 ft., soil the track. I gather that it is believed by those best able to form an opinion that the man is a slaughterer and that he is still within the immediate neighbourhood where his crimes have been committed. If he is a maniac, all his cunning, should he kill another poor creature, will not avail him against the sure hounds that will be laid on his track. Then when London rings the news of his capture, humanity will be under another obligation to the service of man's best friend, the most intelligent of the brute creation, our dogs.

I am Sir, your obedient servant,
George R. Krehl
Kennel Editor to the *Stockkeeper and Fanciers' Chronicle*.

We hear from Mr George R. Krehl that he forgot to mention in his letter that Mr MacKusick has also placed three couples of bloodhounds at the service of the police.

Manchester Courier, October 10th, 1888.

The Whitechapel Tragedies (Extract from letter).

Sir Charles Warren, the Chief Commissioner of the Metropolitan Police is said to be pleased with the result of the trials and if that be so it may be expected that hounds will be brought into use in the event of any mysterious murder. It will be remembered by our readers that a bloodhound was successfully employed in hunting down a murderer in Blackburn, 1876.

A schoolgirl had been outraged and then butchered in the most horrible manner. Part of the remains of the girl were discovered but the police were unable to find either the remainder or the murderer.

The feeling of indignation in *The Times* was so intense that a bloodhound was employed first of all to discover, if possible, the missing parts of the body. The lapse of time had destroyed the scent but the police suspecting two persons took the dog to their houses. At the first of these, the dog displayed no excitement but it had no sooner entered the second than it gave unmistakable evidence of having got upon the scent. It led the police to a fireplace in an upper room and there, up the chimney the police found the head and several bones of a child and part of her clothing. The owner of the house was arrested and afterwards made a full confession of his guilt so that after proper precautions it would appear that the Metropolitan Police have good grounds to hope that aided by the sagacity of bloodhounds, they may yet be able to give a good account of the Whitechapel murders.

Manchester Evening News, October 11th, 1888.

Bloodhounds have actually become a part of our Metropolitan force. The services of two have been secured as Special Constables and go on duty every night. During the day they are kennelled at Kensington and in the evening a couple of policemen may be seen leading them down to the East End where they are kept ready at hand to be put upon the scent of the Whitechapel fiend the moment a fresh murder is discovered.

Truth, October 11th, 1888.

The following story which is worth reproducing at the present moment to show what bloodhounds' keenness of scent is. Captain Norway was murdered on the Turnpike Road between Bodmin and Wadebridge one night nearly 50 years ago. Next morning two bloodhounds belonging to Sir William Molesworth were brought from Pencarrow to the scene of the murder. They followed the scent of the murderers to the estuary of the river Camel where they were checked by the high tide. The tide had been low when the murderers had waded across. The dogs were ferried over the river and recovered the scent which they stuck to till it brought them and the constables to a cottage in which there were two brothers, name of Lightfoot. These men were tried for the murder at Bodmin assizes and duly hung.

Vanity Fair, 17th November, 1888.
Jack the Ripper.

After all the talk about bloodhounds as detectors of crime, after the empty experiments made by Sir Charles Warren himself, and after all the other supposed preparations, the opportunity for the real test of the hounds' utility as a criminal detector has arrived and nothing has been ready. A woman is found murdered and the police keep the scene clear until the bloodhounds shall arrive for it.

It is said that they are being fetched. Presently a messenger arrives to say that the hounds have been countermanded (and after an explanation can be made, the opportunity is gone forever).

Why this farce should have been perpetrated is one of those things which no man can understand. Mr Brough, who's hounds were supposed to be lying in wait, now explains that he had taken them away because as Sir Charles Warren was proposing to try them on burglars he feared less they should be poisoned, in which event he had been unable to get any guarantee that their loss would not fall upon himself.

Whether these hounds are capable of tracking down a murderer or not, I'm not prepared to say but at least they ought to be tried as should every other possible resource when the police are beaten as they are here. They would have at least as good a chance after a murderer as they would after a burglar, but it is all of apiece with our modern methods that a chance which might possibly mean the saving of half a dozen lives, should have been lost because an official has not thought right to guarantee a private individual against the loss of property which he ('the official') was ready to borrow, but apparently unwilling to pay for.

We will never know for sure, but it does seem likely that if the bloodhounds had remained with the police in this case, further murders might have been prevented and the murderer might even have been caught. As it was, the authorities were reluctant to pay for the insurance cover that Edwin Brough required, and the hounds, Barnaby and Burgho, were taken back to Scarborough by their owner without having been given a chance to track 'the Ripper'.

Moving from fact to fiction, it is interesting to note that when Sir Arthur Conan Doyle wrote his memorable Sherlock Holmes story 'The Hound of the Baskervilles', he took his inspiration for the great hound from the special powers of the bloodhound. I understand that he made a careful study of the way the bloodhound works a scent before writing the story, and was able to incorporate details which give the tale life and realism.

Present-day Police Views

While researching for this book I met a number of interesting and helpful people, especially within the police and the army. The following information is extracted from an interview with Chief Inspector Wilkinson of the Metropolitan Police Dog Training Establishment at Keston, Kent, probably the foremost training school of its type in the world, and, as Inspector Wilkinson proudly said, 'Many visitors come from all over the world to attend courses held here'.

Bloodhounds were used in the early days for police work in this country and one was used at the Keston establishment in the early 1950s.

For olfactory scenting the bloodhound is everything that authors, such as Conan Doyle, have implied; they are a very efficient tracking dog. But I think even bloodhound breeders will agree that they do have a natural timidity, which surprises people who, because of the very name bloodhound, think that when they find their quarry they rip them to pieces. It is that timidity in their breeding which makes them unsuitable to us for other aspects of police work.

Our dogs are often described in the media, quite wrongly, as tracker dogs; general purpose police dogs do not only track, they do a variety of exercises: they track, they search, they chase and they stop people, and one dog does all those exercises. In our experience, we have not found a bloodhound that can do all those aspects of police work, and bloodhounds are not prominent in civilian working trials in the Police Dog Stakes, Working Dog Stakes, or, in fact, the Utility Stakes. There is a sad absence, I think you will agree, of the breed. Although you have your own trials stakes, these, I believe, deal mainly with tracking, but the stakes I have just mentioned, include a variety of other things. I don't suppose that bloodhound breeders would want their hounds to do 'man work' because that would do away with their natural breeding line and inherent traits.

Dogs used for modern police work are not used in the same way as, for example, the dogs or hounds used in the days of 'Jack the Ripper'. Dogs used during that period were used usually on an aid basis by the person who owned the hounds. A private individual

Following a savage attack and robbery at Hucklesbrook near the New Forest in the 1930s, the police called upon a local bloodhound owner, J. Chamberlain, for help in tracing the attacker. Mr Chamberlain's two hounds gave valuable assistance to the police in this case as on several other occasions.

who had a tracking dog would be summoned by the local constabulary and asked if they could be of assistance solely for tracking from A to B. The person handling the dog was not a policeman and had no police powers.

You could suggest that that was the beginning of the seed being sown in police minds about using dogs, but I wouldn't like to say that this was definitely the origin. The seed remained dormant for a long time before the police in this country tried, in the 1930s to experiment with the use of dogs in police service. That was discontinued in 1939 at the outbreak of war but was tried again around 1946–47, when pilot schemes were set up. You could say that the birth of the police dog was as short a time ago as 1946–47.

The multi-purpose roles that today's police dog has to cope with, originated from those pioneering days of the late 1940s. Policemen were allowed to take dogs on duty with them on their night beat at various times in the history of the police service but only as a companion or a possible deterrent. It was his own dog and could have been any breed, probably quite a few were mongrels and quite good too, some of them. They were useful in as much as that they could bark and act as a deterrent, but for tracking, seeking and chasing a criminal, they were not very good.

We mainly use the German shepherd dog for general police work now, also some Labradors, some Rottweilers, Dobermans and Weimaraners. In fact, we have a Weimaraner at present, which is an outstanding police dog on the streets and an outstanding trials dog. Of course, with all these breeds you have to be selective, but in some of the breeds there is not sufficient number to select from a wide choice.

The Rottweiler has been used quite a lot on the Continent, and we use some of them here. They are big, powerful, strong and agile working dogs.

It is very difficult to compare the olfactory senses or the physical powers of some of these breeds. The dog that you select must be up to scratch and, of course, you're not only dealing with the dog, but also the handler, who is just as complicated and the two make up the one team. You can have the finest dog in the world, but if you give it to an indifferent handler, you won't get the best results. On the other hand you can have a dog with less qualities than some, but give it to a good handler and he will extract from that dog every quality that the dog possesses.

In our specialist role we have dogs that are specialist for narcotics, others that are specialised in searching for explosives. To date, we use Labradors for these purposes because they have the inherent retrieving capability and the physical ability and temperament required.

Another important point is that the Labrador is socially acceptable; more so than a German shepherd dog in many places. In fact, the Labradors have all the physical capabilities that you need in a police dog: they are as strong as the German shepherd and some of the best police dogs that I have ever had the pleasure of working with have been of this breed. In fact, one of our champion dogs for many years was a dog called Bonny, handled by P.C. Fleet of Croydon. Sadly now dead, she was for many years one of the finest police dogs in the country – powerful bite – beautiful tracker – beautiful searching dog.

In answering the question, 'Why are bloodhounds not used more to find lost children?', the answer, in my opinion, is this: if you are faced with the choice between a bloodhound and a German shepherd, the olfactory capabilities of a German shepherd are every bit as good as those of a bloodhound – there is no scientific dispute to that – but the German shepherd is also a multi-role dog. As policemen, we may be seeking a lost child one day, and tracking a violent criminal who has decamped across the fields with a shotgun the next. Clearly, a bloodhound is fine for tracking a child, but when it comes to chasing and apprehending, it would not rise to the task. Since it is impractical to keep one dog for tracking children and another for all other tasks, we do not use bloodhounds at all.

In police work you need a dog which can fulfil all roles and we have found, and it is accepted internationally, that in the German shepherd you have such a dog. It has the physique, it has the olfactory capabilities, it has the nobility of appearance to give it a very strong deterrent value. The bloodhound is a beautiful tracking dog, but it is a lovable creature; can you imagine the lack of effect that it would have in patrolling rowdy areas, in comparison to the German shepherd?

Another point to bear in mind is that of economics, which must inevitably be taken into account when training police dogs. I cannot experiment with just any dog. Let us take a poodle, for example: without disrespect to them, on the whole, they do not make satisfactory police dogs. If I said that it was completely impossible to train one, I expect that someone, somewhere would produce one. However, that would simply be one poodle in many, and in the end, I have to consider the economic factors in the training of a police dog.

I would say that with regard to the some 8000 arrests we made last year, about 40% of those were tracking jobs. But you must remember that we train our dogs to investigate the ground thoroughly when on a track, searching for clues. Unlike your bloodhound trials where you allow your hound to go as fast as it likes, we would very much frown on this in competition work and the dog would be heavily penalised for doing so, as this would make it impossible to pick up any clues that may be scattered *en route*, such as articles of clothing, or even valuables that may have been discarded. Furthermore, a policeman who has run a mile or so to keep up with his dog would not be in a very good physical shape to deal with any desperado that may be at the other end of the trail. When tracking, our ideal is a fast walking pace with a nice slack tracking line, indicating that the dog is properly on the track, his nose to the ground. That is what we call tracking.

When considering the question of scent, the dog is aided by two things: air and ground scent. We train our dogs when tracking (not hunting) to hunt ground scent, which is that made by the impact of the foot on the ground – crushed vegetation, the smell of the boot polish on the footware, etc. There is also air scent which theoretically flows from the body and comes down rather like smoke or fog, and lingers, but eventually drifts away.

We train dogs throughout the police service to track on ground scent and we do this in the very early stages of training by tracking down wind, because otherwise the dog will take the airborne scent. But if you track down wind, after a short time the wind will have blown away the air scent, which enables the dog to track specifically on ground scent. If the ground temperature is higher than the air temperature, we know that we have a better track, allowing, of course, for other factors such as sunlight.

When leaving here, a dog is trained to be able to track a soft surface track for up to two hours and on its passing out test is likely to have a mile track. It has been worked out over the years that a two-hour-old track is about the maximum amount of time you would have before anyone in this country would be well and truly away from the scene. A mile is chosen simply as a reasonable distance to test the dog, though we do tracks of three or four miles to test endurance, but we do these for the same reason you perform your own trials and only when there is enough time and space to do that. You may be testing six dogs in a class, which limits the amount of time and space available. I might add that a considerable thanks goes to our local farmers in allowing us to use their land.

When a dog is hunting, i.e. taking an air scent, he does that in what we call a search exercise. When we send a dog to find a person, he would be involved in what we describe as quartering; going from left to right through a wood or wherever (not tracking, but searching). His olfactory senses, his ears and, to some extent, his eyes are used. This exercise might well be employed where there has been a break-in in, for example, a large department store and the criminals are still in the building. We have known our dogs follow an air scent in the open air for a distance of some 150 paces, homing-in like an arrow.

One of the most important things to bear in mind when training our dogs, and our instructors echo this time and time again to handlers, is 'Have confidence in your dog'. For the handlers who can read their dogs well and do not pull their dogs off a scent either in competition or operational field work, are the ones who will have success nine times out of ten.

It might be interesting to note that bloodhounds are used in the Israeli Police Force, solely for tracking of course. I have recently come back from there and I found that they have crossed them with Dobermans. I saw these crosses working and they were reasonable, but I thought they would have been better had they kept to a pure breed. However, they have got some very healthy and fit bloodhounds out there.

The following extract on the subject of scent, is taken from a police pamphlet 'Police Dogs, Training and Care'.

Scent
1. The dog, like most animals, in its wild state depended to a large extent on its nose for survival and it is a scientific fact that a dog has a sense of smell immeasurably keener than that of a human being. Use of this characteristic is the means by which a dog is able, under certain conditions, to follow a trail.

2. The theory of scent is a wide and complex subject but for practical police purposes may be divided into broad categories as follows:
   (i) Ground scent; and
   (ii) Wind scent.

Ground Scent

3. Ground scent which is followed by the dog in tracking, is caused by contact with the ground resulting in disturbance. The slightest movement of the soil or the crushing of grass, other vegetation and insect life, leaves particles and/or drops of moisture lying on the ground, all of which give off a scent and thus denote a trail. Some of this scent will obviously adhere to the crushing instrument, e.g. the footwear, and may be carried in this way for some distance from one type of ground to another. Experience has shown that the dog depends to a large extent on this effect from crushing in following a track.

Wind Borne Scent

4. Wind scent is the name given to the scent which attracts the dog in searching. It is air borne from the individual or object and may, in the former case, be described as the personal odour from the body of the person concerned; in the latter it may be characteristic to the object or may be the result of some previous human contact. The scent of the article itself may be alien to the particular ground on which it lies, e.g. a piece of sawn or broken wood lying on grassland. The amount of personal odour varies according to constitution, health, clothing, nourishment, activity, mental condition and state of cleanliness. It is greatly intensified when there is physical exertion.

5. Wind scent may also include occupational odours carried in the clothing of the wearer. In some circumstances they may be very characteristic and distinctive.

6. The dog using its acute sense of smell becomes conscious of the scent through the air it breathes. The degree of discernment therefore varies with the concentration of the scent which in turn varies with the rate of evaporation, air movement and type of country over which the scent is set up. Quite obviously the most important feature affecting scent from an operational

point of view is time. The more quickly a dog can be brought to follow a scent the more successful the result is likely to be.

Factors affecting Scent

7. Scent is subject to evaporation and is therefore greatly affected by climatic conditions. Generally speaking scenting conditions are most favourable:
   (i) in mild, dull weather;
   (ii) when the temperature of the ground is higher than the air, i.e., normally at night time;
   (iii) in areas where the ground is sheltered.
8. Factors which adversely affect scent are:
   (i) hot sunshine;
   (ii) strong winds;
   (iii) heavy rainfall after the scent has been set up.
9. Frost and snow may have either the effect of preserving or destroying a scent depending on whether this occurs before or after the scent has been occasioned.
10. Pedestrian or vehicular traffic will quickly disperse a scent.
11. The foregoing, already described as a wide and complex subject, is one which must be interpreted with great care when working a dog under practical conditions. There will be innumerable occasions when the accepted theories are contradicted by the dog's ability and willingness to follow a scent which under accepted conditions should be non-existent. The only true test is for the dog to be given the opportunity to establish whether or not working conditions prevail.

Present-day Army Views

One of the most interesting days I spent in researching this book was that at the Royal Army Veterinary Corps (R.A.V.C.) Training Centre at Melton Mowbray in Leicestershire with their commandant, Lieutenant-Colonel Keith Morgan Jones. It was a particularly good day to visit as it was during the annual Army dog trials which not only allowed me to see some action but also to talk to a number of trainers and handlers who had first hand experience of using dogs and bloodhounds in military work.

Naturally, much of the current activity is classified information and consequently not for open discussion. However, there were a number of interesting stories which I heard and one or two I have related here.

According to Colonel Morgan Jones, bloodhounds have been used by the British Army in campaigns in such disparate areas as Kenya, Cyprus and Northern Ireland. In tropical and sub-tropical countries they were limited by the climate, although they produced some good results against Mau-Mau and EOKA terrorists. This limitation came as a result of persistent skin trouble due to the heat.

Used by the army in support of the police, bloodhounds, although primarily used in the delayed pursuit of suspect terrorists, by virtue of their exceptional olfactory powers, proved extremely valuable in ancillary ways. Many things discarded or hidden by fleeing suspects were indicated by bloodhounds, despite the fact that they were not trained to find them. These included weapons, ammunition and articles of clothing, all of which provided valuable forensic evidence. Further forensic evidence included such clues as footprints and tyre marks (at the end of a track when a suspect was picked up by car) from which casts could be taken.

Some typical incidents would include remarks in the reports such as:

> 'After shooting of two members of the security forces, dog tasked 30 minutes later to track gunman. Track (back track from firepoint) of 300 metres to hide in bushes. Found 57 rounds of ammunition.'
>
> 'After shots fired at house of politician, dog tasked seven and a half hours later. After false start at estimated fire point the dog was cast 100 metres beyond. After track of 200 metres dog indicated on three rounds, one live, two spent and then tracked a further 100 metres across a field up a road to a lane where fresh tyre marks were found.'
>
> 'Following a shooting incident, dog picked up scent and tracked 600 metres along a railway line. The track led to a group of shanties. Dog tracked to a particular shanty where the occupant,

who possessed an old rifle, was arrested by the police. Track 24 hours cold.'

The colonel went on to say:

Five bloodhounds have been procured for the army up to as little as three or four years ago and they performed some outstanding scenting feats. However, they were not necessarily useful for all the purposes that the army required.

We've been using them for many, many years, dating back to World War I when they, and other dogs, were conscripted into the army because there was no breeding programme in times of war. There was quite a selection of dogs brought in, including Airedales and Rottweilers and even the odd Doberman as well as bloodhounds. Since that time the bloodhound has been found to be exceptionally good for tracking: this is what they were bred for in the first place and I must admit they were very, very good trackers.

So, in campaigns such as Cyprus, Malaya, Mau-Mau in Kenya, and, of course, latterly in Northern Ireland, as long as there was nobody shooting or laying booby traps for the soldiers, they were ideal because they had an exceptionally good nose. However, like any other hound they tended to be difficult to train and during the latter campaign we found that we had to have dogs that were obedient and disciplined and that could be pulled up at a particular point so that they would not compromise the men, or themselves, by not being under control. As I said earlier, bloodhounds are all nose and no brain; that is the unfortunate characteristic that goes with the breed.

Within the army there is this acceptance of standardisation, and Alsatians (German shepherd dogs) and Labradors have been our accepted dogs for both the routine and the specialist tasks. I don't think that either the Alsatian or the Labrador has as good a nose as the average bloodhound, but, as we mentioned earlier, bloodhounds have these two major problems of skin disease and lack of discipline. For operational reasons we have now stopped using them altogether but it is possible that they will come back again if we need action for criminal work in a quiet environment. In fact this is where, in my opinion, they could prove very useful – where there is no danger of someone leaving a booby trap or a bomb behind or shooting at the handler.

We have had incidents where a bloodhound has actually gone in, having tracked a criminal or suspect, and winkled him out himself. But you generally find, more often than not, that he will go in and lick the bloke all over saying 'Jolly nice, Sir, to see you. Haven't I been a clever fellow?'.

Another point to bear in mind is that of transportation. The biggest of our Alsatians is about 100 lb [45 kg] in weight and this is considerably lighter than some of the present-day bloodhounds which may weigh as much as some 130 lb [59 kg]. However, I have never heard of this being the reason for eliminating the bloodhound from military operations, since forms of transportation such as helicopters could ably cope with a bloodhound. I do not ever recall instances where hounds were considered to have suspect temperament in getting in and out of helicopters, and we found the average temperament of a bloodhound is that of a good natured fool. In fact we had one in Northern Ireland we called Buffoon. Probably more to the point is that although bloodhounds may be considered untrainable for many of our disciplines, they could well be said to have a strong single-mindedness. It is a fact that for a straight track from A to B ignoring other factors for a moment, the bloodhound is 100% the most able. This is how we have used them and possibly will use them again. We have had some excellent tracks that started down tarmac roads, across fields, through backyards and eventually ended catching the fellow in his lounge.

I can also imagine a role for bloodhounds in casualty detection where chaps are buried by fallen masonry after bombardment or bombing, or have been injured from parachute drops. I am convinced that the bloodhound is one of the best breeds for finding such persons.

With regard to scenting, if you look at it objectively, there is no such thing as ground scent being detected by a dog, because no dog goes round physically with its nose on the ground all the time – it would be worn down to a stump in no time at all. All that scent on the ground is evaporating and becoming air scent and I think bloodhounds are just like any other dog. They will pick it up eight paces off-track because the wind is blowing it there, especially the characters that go at 30 miles an hour, they're not worried particularly about it being grass. They have got the main concentration and in a 25 knot wind that will be all of some eight paces away.

All our dogs are trained on scent, whatever job we are doing.

Analysis of scent can be done in a number of ways. We have talked about two ways of analysing it, namely, ground scent and air scent, but we also go for another classification of scent factors in the service and that is: the smell of an object itself; the smell of chemicals associated with the object; the smell of a human association with an object; and lastly, the disturbance of the environment. Now the smell of the object itself in cases of bloodhound tracking is the same as for the other three and that is the smell of the human it is going for. But the chemicals are still there, e.g. the aftershave fragrance, boot polish and the clothes and what have you.

I am quite convinced that the most important factor in searching and in tracking is the disturbance of the environment, i.e. the crushing of the grass on earth etc., by the footfall of the quarry. We have seen this in the search dogs: if somebody has opened a drawer just before search, the dog goes straight in and straight to that drawer because the dust of the woodwork has been exposed for a short time. I have got a picture of a German contraption from World War I, which consists of a big wheel with wooden feet on it. This did not depend on human quarry. All it was was something to run across a field to disturb the environment.

One might say that the scent picked up by a dog or hound which has blown some distance, is in fact a mixture of body scent and crushed vegetation. You might also consider the question of people thinking that there is not much scent left behind if the quarry is wearing gum-boots – well, don't you believe it! There is a tremendous amount still coming through as far as a dog's senses are concerned. We've done all sorts of experiments and gum-boots are as pervious as other footwear. We have wrapped up scents for fourteen days in polythene and the dog has still been able to indicate it after about an hour cold. I also firmly believe that no chemical, fertilizer for example, can mask a scent for long. It may cause the dog or hound some discomfort but no more than that, and will not really detract from the four factors which go to make up the scent picture.

When I went to the Sergeants' Mess, I was able to have a long and interesting talk with Ex-Sergeant Major George Yeandle B.E.M., Chief dog trainer for the Royal Army Veterinary Corps. He had the following to say:

In about 1970 the army wanted tracking dogs, and as our last brush was in Borneo around 1964, there were only a few trained tracking dogs around to be used in teaching young trainers how to track. Since the requirement was then quite urgent, we had a conference – Captain Deacon, Sergeant Major Aimes and myself – and I suggested that it might be an idea to try bloodhounds again. You see, we had two bloodhounds before, although I never saw them being trained back in 1959, and they were left over from trouble that had occurred earlier. There was not much at that time that they were needed for operationally and so I was given the task of looking after them. As it happened, I fell in love with these two hounds. I loved the way they tracked – they just hunted on and cast about. There was one – he was a real terror – if he came to a fence and found he couldn't get over, he would work himself up into such a state that if you tried to help him he would turn on you. The only thing you could do was let go of the leash, let him find his own way through and then clamber after him. These two hounds were not to be fooled around, but nevertheless I developed quite a soft spot for them. I had previously read Colonel Richardson's book *War, Police and Watch Dogs*, from World War 1 and it captured my imagination with regard to bloodhounds. Although the general opinion was that they were not up to much – they couldn't do this and they couldn't do that – I always felt that someone who cared for them would extract some qualities of real value from them.

Anyway, when, nearly ten years later, this opportunity arose, I said 'let's get some bloodhounds'. Captain Deacon had an open mind to try them out and so it fell upon me and the Sergeant Major to go along to a bloodhound trial to see them working and then produce a report. So we went down to the New Forest, we watched the hounds tracking and were very impressed with them. We perhaps had some reservation with regard to some of the handling but on the whole felt if they were a little better controlled they would be really good.

We eventually contacted a breeder and took two hounds on approval. We had with us an old saloon car and stuck these two great things in the back. I suppose they would have been between twelve months and two years old and were very big. We got them back and I was given the responsibility to train them. Gerry and Lombard were their names. The first time I started to try and walk Gerry up the road, he threw himself down and just lay there. So I

Ex-Sergeant Major George Yeandle B.E.M., Chief Army Dog Trainer and Instructor at the Royal Army Veterinary Corps with Barnaby.

put the lead over my shoulder and just carried on walking, dragging him for about a hundred paces. Eventually he got up and shook himself and never ever gave any more trouble, he just walked with me after that.

We then started basic tracking training, treating them as we would do any other dog: two people making a big fuss, one standing and the other going off and dropping into dead ground. It was then just a matter of making the track longer and colder. There was no shortage of people walking lines and in three months they were tracking three and four hours cold without any problem. That was hard surface tracking over roads, up over the top of slag heaps etc.

We tried them on obedience training. But it didn't really work. They would walk to heel, stand still when you stood still but that was about it. However, they would live with a man in a billet, fitting in and keeping out of the way.

The eyes were a constant problem – always running. The veterinary surgeons here would cut a piece out and stitch them and they would look good, but three weeks later they were back down again because there was so much wrinkle on them.

We said that we wanted to keep both of them as they were excellent trackers but the vet noticed the fluid in Lombard's eye and we were forced to return him to the kennels.

The army then acquired three further hounds. I wasn't involved in that selection but one of our chaps went to get them. These were Buffoon, Solomon and Barnaby, and so we eventually ended up with four hounds. These hounds were fantastic and the chaps who handled them were bloodhound barmy – once they had one they did not want to go back to other dogs.

As soon as they had finished preliminary training the hounds were taken out on military work, straight onto the streets tracking. On one occasion, a car was stopped at a road block, the doors flew open, two chaps jumped out (I believe they had weapons) and just ran off across a road, over a field and away. The soldiers lost sight of them and so they called out one of the bloodhounds, Gerry, some two or three hours later. They cast him on the road, he picked up the track, put his nose down like a vacuum cleaner and found two blokes behind the bushes – some top people required by the authorities so I believe.

Another time, a woman who had been very depressed

disappeared and the local authorities, having heard that we had bloodhounds, asked us if we would travel up to them and use one on this case. From all accounts, the handler arrived on the scene (which, incidentally, was a council estate), cast the hound around, picked up a line and off he went. He eventually took the handler to a big reservoir. The authorities claimed that it was out of the question that the woman was so distressed that she would have ended up in the reservoir and that it was simply the bloodhound going for a drink. They went back to the house and cast the animal again, and they ended up back down by the water. This seemed to convince them that maybe the hound was right, so they put some divers in and found her body in the water, right at the spot where the hound had stopped tracking.

On another occasion, a bloodhound (Barnaby) was in a particularly hostile area and was being walked along a patrol. The idea was, that because all dog handlers are fully trained soldiers they could be tagged onto the end of a fighting patrol. They were going over a bridge, when suddenly the hound shot to one side to go under the bridge. Obviously the handler thought that he had picked up game and so he pulled him back, but the hound had actually found a big 800 lb bomb under the bridge. How he found it, because they weren't trained to the scent of explosives, I don't know. It might have been the scent of somebody planting it there or simply a foreign scent of explosives which he thought 'That's a strange smell, I've never smelt that before. Let me go and have a look'. But he went and looked and found the bomb and the patrol thought this was wonderful.

Buffoon went to a stout, very straight thinking sort of chap and he treated him just the same as any of the other dogs he handled. Buffoon was a big red dog whom we had tried to obedience train. He would walk along and sit or stop when you stopped, but that was it. However, his handler was with a detachment somewhat isolated from the rest of us, and when I went up there one day, I was surprised, to say the least, when he demonstrated obedience with this big hound. He managed to get it to heel, sit, stay, and stay while he walked away in a great big circle until he said 'Heel', when the hound would come up to heel. Now, we are supposed to be experts here and we couldn't get anywhere near that standard with our 'bloods'. Obviously, because this chap would not accept that there was anything special about a bloodhound, he managed to train Buffoon just like any other dog. The hound, however, was very aggressive and would not let anyone else handle him. If you gave him a veterinary inspection he had to be muzzled and firmly held because he'd tear you limb from limb. In fact, he was not the sort of brute to meet on a dark night.

Of the two other hounds, Barnaby was gentle, he could track, he would get into anything in the way of transport that you asked him to. In fact, he was the one hound I would have liked to have taken home.

The bloods were very big, and when he stood on his hind legs, Buffoon was nearly as tall as me and I'm six foot one. They weighed in at about 110 lb [50 kg] plus but never carried any surplus flesh and they were very fit because of the amount of work they did. Their great problem was skin trouble, i.e. eczema and messy eyes. You can't say they were not looked after, the men would always be cleaning and brushing them. However, they would be sitting around, getting in and out of trucks, getting grit from the side of the road and so on. It's not quite the same life as they would have with the average domestic owner. The men looked after them well, but at the same time they worked them hard.

The bloodhounds held the fort very well during the period while we trained and built up our supply of trained Labradors and German shepherds.

Don't get the idea it's just bloods that did these wonderful tracks. There were shepherds and Labradors too, but the bloods did the job, and the important thing was that they trained so quickly. You might spend six months training a Labrador to track but with the manpower facilities we've got here, in six months a bloodhound was a really top notch dog. They could track down roads, up the side of slag heaps that were all fallen down on four-hour cold lines.

There is no doubt that everyone was very impressed with the way they tracked and right up until the time they had veterinary problems they were tolerated. If people suddenly ask for two tracking dogs to stand by and we say that we can only supply one, the reaction is, 'Well, according to the information we've got, there are three in our brigade', and I would have to reply that two were sick and unfit for duty. This, as you can imagine, did not go down too well.

I believe there may well be the case for more selective breeding of the bloodhound and, at the risk of upsetting traditionalists, I would like something more like a foxhound – strong, able to jump, go over stone walls, nice tight eyes; in fact, if you could keep the nose and the ability to track and change the machine that carries it, this is what I would like. You see, I believe that much of the trouble stems from hounds being reared for the show ring although I'm the first to admit that I am not an expert in bloodhounds – I just like them. But I do feel that the physical problems we have experienced are only going to get worse in the hound rather than get better, unless more care is taken in breeding.

At this point we were joined in the mess by a number of trainer/handlers and there was a good deal of laughter when the subject of walking a line wearing Wellington boots was mentioned. The army's comment was that they lived in wellingtons for a large part of their training and that this did not make the slightest difference to either the hounds' or dogs' ability in finding scent. In fact nearly all their practice lines were walked in boots.

One handler made the following comments:

> I have found bloodhounds very possessive. I never found them any problem with regards to transportation, but they are a bit wary of cover, i.e. brambles and thorns, where a Labrador would not bother so much. Because a 'blood' will find it a little more difficult than other dogs to get over obstacles, this can sometimes be a strong indication as to where the line has actually gone, for if he does persevere on the same spot, you know you're onto something. I would say the best tracking bloodhound we had was Solomon without a doubt. He was a big dog, probably the biggest and most powerful of all those that we had at that time.
>
> Buffoon also did some excellent work. You probably heard the case which is on the operation reports where there was a track and the police dog, a German shepherd, was called in and wouldn't let the army dog work. He made a complete mess of the track. Then they decided to let the army dog work and he successfully tracked ten hours later, after the police dog and all the people had been over the ground. That was one of the best tracks that I have ever seen.
>
> Of course, you must remember that a dog or hound may do an excellent track and arrive at the end of the correct line only to find

that the culprit has gone – into a car or whatever. This goes down as a negative report, but you can never prove that someone hasn't been there. It is possible that 90% of our tracks come to nothing, but what it does is to build up a plan of the way people are using certain routes and this knowledge is invaluable.

I found my conversation with these people extremely valid, for, although it was accompanied with a good sense of humour, it was not a game or sport to them, but a responsible job of work. They were the ones who selected animals for their ability, knowing that lives may depend on their performance.

Having spoken at length to the military, police officials, and those people that have hunted for sport most of their lives, I believe I have gathered together a spectrum of knowledgeable opinions on the use of the bloodhound as a working animal that, although controversial, will remain an interesting comment on the breed.

Postscript

There is little doubt that if you already hunt you do not need me to comment on the excitement to be enjoyed in the field. But if you do so and have not yet observed the bloodhound working a cold line on a good scenting day, I venture to suggest that there is still an exciting hunting experience if you feel so inclined.

On the other hand if there are those who know little of the hunt and have found this book sufficient stimulus to want to know more, then I will be happy that I have helped to be instrumental in introducing them to a sport that could bring years of enjoyment of hounds and the natural environment in which we live.

Appendix 1: Kennel Club Working Trial Rules for Bloodhounds

1. *Entries:* Bloodhounds must be named at the time of making the entries and particulars given in accordance with Kennel Club Working Trial Rule No. 1.
2. *Order of running:* At a date prior to the meeting, previously announced, a draw shall take place to determine the order in which the hounds shall be run. By mutual agreement, owners may vary the order of running, subject to the approval of the stewards.
3. *Disqualification for absence:* The Committee shall announce the hour for beginning each day, and each hound must be brought up in its proper turn without delay. If absent for more than half-an-hour when called, a hound shall be liable to be disqualified by the Judge or Judges.
4. *Method of working:* Hounds must be handled by their owners or their deputies. All hounds entered in any one stake shall be tried in the same way.
5. *Kennel Club Working Trial Certificate:* A Kennel Club Working Trial Certificate will be awarded to a bloodhound winning a Senior Stake without assistance at a Championship Working Trial for Bloodhounds if it has clearly identified the runner to the satisfaction of the Judge or Judges.

A hound will be considered to have made a satisfactory identification if it is seen to approach and clearly select the runner from a group of three people at the end of the line.

Conditions:

1. Only Bloodhounds holding a Bloodhound Club or Association of Bloodhound Breeders' Full Working Certificate or Permit (i.e. certified to be free from riot with farm stock) may be hunted free. Hounds running on a Restricted Permit or Working Certificate must be leashed. Handlers must not under any circumstances drop the leash or otherwise release the hound at any time during the progress of their hunt, or they shall be liable to disqualification by the Judge.
2. These Trials are held under Kennel Club Working Trial Rules and Regulations and a Kennel Club Working Trial Certificate for Bloodhounds may be awarded to the winner of the Senior Stake.
3. *Entries:* Bloodhounds may be entered in one stake only that being the lowest stake for which they are eligible at the closing date for entries.
   Nominations: Bloodhounds may be nominated in the stake immediately above that for which they are entered, provided they have previously gained a second place in that stake.
4. A. *Novice Stake:* For bloodhounds holding A.B.B. or B.C. Working Certificates or current A.B.B. or B.C. Working Permits at the close of entries. No hound that has won a Novice Stake or been placed 1st, 2nd or 3rd in an A.B.B. or B.C. Senior, Intermediate or Junior Stake may enter in this stake.
    B. *Junior Stake:* For bloodhounds that have held an A.B.B. or B.C. *FULL* Working Certificate, who have won 1st or 2nd in an A.B.B. or B.C. Novice Stake at the close of entries. No hound who has won an A.B.B. or B.C. Junior, Intermediate or Senior Stake may enter in this stake.
    C. *Intermediate Stake:* For bloodhounds that have won 1st or 2nd in an A.B.B. or B.C. Junior Stake at the close of entries. No hound that has won an A.B.B. or B.C. Intermediate or Senior Stake may enter in this stake.
    D. *Senior Stake:* For bloodhounds that have won 1st or 2nd in an A.B.B. or B.C. Intermediate Stake.

5. *Fees:* All entries and nominations must be accompanied by the appropriate fees which must be received by the closing date for entries. A draw will be made from among the nominations should these exceed the vacancies in a Stake. Should a vacancy for a nomination not occur, the nomination fee will be refunded in full. No fees will be refunded in the case of withdrawal or non-attendance by a competitor.
6. The Committee will not be responsible for any claim for injury or compensation occasioned by or arising out of these Trials.
7. Owners of Bloodhounds at Trials will be liable for any damage they may do. Any hound chasing or injuring livestock may be refused entry or required to hunt on a leash at any future Trial, such a condition to be imposed at the discretion of the Committee.
8. Should a judge be unable to fulfil his engagement, the Committee reserves the right to appoint a substitute.
9. A line may only be re-laid at the sole discretion of the judge.
10. Runners will be expected to be at the end of their lines ready for identification for a maximum period after the scheduled start of:
Novice Stake – $\frac{3}{4}$ hour Intermediate – $1\frac{3}{4}$ hours
Junior Stake – $1\frac{1}{4}$ hours Senior Stake – $2\frac{1}{4}$ hours
unless specifically requested by the steward to remain longer.

Appendix 2:
Some Useful Addresses

The Association of Bloodhound Breeders
Hon. Secretary   Mrs Priscilla Bingham
                              220 Hurn Road
                              Ringwood
                              Hants

The Bloodhound Club
Hon. Secretary   Mrs Bobbie Edwards
                              68 Fellows Road
                              London NW3

The Kennel Club of Great Britain
                              1 Clarges Street
                              Piccadilly
                              London W17 8AB

The American Bloodhound Club
Secretary (Corresponding)   Mrs Ruth G. Anderson
                              4 North, 730 Brookside West
                              St Charles
                              Ill. 60174, USA

The Bloodhound Association of Victoria
Secretary   Mrs Gwenda O'Dwyer
                              29 Allens Road
                              Heathmont 3135
                              Victoria, Australia

Glossary

Babble: to give tongue idly on scent other than that of the quarry.
Bloat: gastric torsion – distension of the stomach often with a twist of the stomach.
Body scent: scent that falls from the body.
Brace: two matched dogs of the same breed.
Cast: to circle round looking for the scent.
Champion (Sh): hound which has won three Kennel Club Challenge Certificates at shows.
Champion (WT): hound which has won two Kennel Club Working Trial Certificates.
Change: to start onto a scent other than that of the quarry.
Check: to stop and verify the line.
Clean eye: not weeping, infected or watering; not invaded by wrinkle or eyelash.
Close country: closely wooded country.
Coldness of a line: time lapse between runner starting and hound being laid on.
Cover: woods or undergrowth which conceal game.
Cowhocked: hocks turned inwards.
Dead ground: ground below the level of other ground so that it is out of sight.
Dew claw: rudimentary inner toe of a dog's foot.
Dewlap: loose pendulous skin under the throat.
Drag: scent laid by artificial means.
Draghounds: hounds which hunt an artificial scent laid by a trailing object such as aniseed etc.

Entropion: condition in which the eye lid and lashes turn in on the eyeball.
Feather: to wave the stern when picking up the scent.
Flews: pendulous inner corners of the upper lips.
Foil: a scent over that of the quarry.
Free from change: a hound free from change will not change from the hunted scent to a fresh one.
Handler: the person accompanying the hound, to assist or guide the hound should he need help. Huntsman.
Harefoot: a long, narrow foot.
Heel line: the line in the reverse direction.
Hip displasia: condition in which the head of femur is not wholly within the hip socket.
Hock: the 'ankle' joint of the hind leg (the joint between the stifle and the foot).
Hound: a dog used in hunting, especially in hunting by scent.
Hunted free: off a leash.
Hunt the clean boot: to follow the natural scent of man without any artificial aids.
Knuckled-up foot: tight foot, not spread out.
Lay on: to start the hound or hounds on the scent.
Lift: to take a hound off the line he is hunting.
Limiers: hounds led on a line or leash when nearing the quarry.
Line: trail of scent left by the quarry.
Mark: to indicate a spot or object that contains the quarry's scent (e.g. a hound might put his paws up on a gate that the quarry has crossed, i.e. mark the gate).
Mute: silent.
Pastern: lower part of dog's leg, between the hock and paw.
Own the line: to be settled on the line and working on the scent.
Quarry: the person (runner) or animal that the hound is hunting.
Rangy: tall and long.
Read: to understand what the hound is doing, i.e. casting on the scent etc., by watching his actions.
Regain the line: to find the scent after losing it.
Riot: to hunt anything other than the original quarry.
Runner: quarry.

Settle on the line: to be steadily hunting the scent.
Smeller: the article of clothing etc. left by the runner as the clue for the hound.
Speak: to give tongue.
Steady: to keep constantly on the line.
Stifle: the 'knee joint' of the hind leg (the joint between the hip and hock).
Track: to follow a trail using visual and other aids.
Tongue, to give or throw: to use voice.

Index

Numbers in *italics* refer to pages containing illustrations.

Abingerwood Lime Tree
    Pendragon 15, 27, 33
Absentees 124
Accommodation 121
Accuracy 130–31
Aggression 52
American Foxhound 17
Ardennes 2, 17
Army dogs 210–21
Association of Bloodhound
    Breeders (A.B.B.) 16, 18, 19,
    105, 168, 171, 228
Assyrian dogs 2, *3*

Barnaby (Army hound) *216*,
    217–19
Barnaby (Brough's hound) *195*,
    198, 199, 202
Barsheen Bynda of Hugenot 15
    Ozannah de la Meutre
    d'Autrefois 15, 33
Beaufoy, Mark 17, 192
Bedding 45–6, 51
Belladonna, Ch. 13, 17
Bentinck, Sir Henry 173
Berkeley, Hon. Crantley 10
Bloat 35, 45, 48, 79, 169, 176
Bloodhound Club 34, 105, 140,
    158, 171, 228

Boots, rubber 139, 144, 159, 220
Boravin Fusilier 53, *135*
Borwick, Major 147, 152, 153
Bravo 13, 17
Brighton's Noble Manner
    (Luke) 68, *131*
Brough, Edwin 1, 8, 17, *19*, 21,
    74, 185, 193
    comment by 10, 12, 13, 16,
    180
    views on outcross 79, 177
Brough Records 179–202
    Trophy *30*, 107
Brudenell Bruce, Lady
    Rosemary 171–73
Buchanan-Jardine, Sir John 14,
    178
Buchanan-Jardine, Sir
    Rupert 156, 178
Budgett, H. M. 65
Burgho *195*, *198*, 199, 202
Buxhall Anna, WT Ch. 25, 30,
    31, *42*

Cancer 35
Cardigan, Earl of 171, *172*
Carrington, Lord 9
Casting 61–3, 132, 167
Castle Milk Horsa 14, 17

232

Catalogues 120
Certificate of Merit 107
Chamberlain, J. *204*
Championship Certificate 75
Change, freedom from 10, 67, 128–29, 167
Chase's Mimsy of Brighton, The 15
Cheyenne of Brighton, Ch. The 14, 17, 28, 29, 31, 32
Choosing a puppy 39–45
Coat 35
Collar 54, *61*, 69
Colour 83, 85
Conan Doyle, Sir Arthur 202, 203
Confidence 62, 63, 133
Coral of Westsummerland, Ch. 14, 17, 23, 25
Cottesbrooke Estate 146–51
Countess 13
Couple Stake 20
Cowhocked *88*, *92*
Crease, Jane 146, 150
Crossed lines 59, 67–8, 166
Croup *88*, *90*, *98*, *99*
Cuban Bloodhound 12, 192, 194

Deer 9, 10, 13, 64, 178
Delburn Buccaneer, Ch. 14, 17
Dew claws 157
Diana, Ch. 13, 17
Discipline 52–3
Diverging line 67
Dog or bitch, choosing between 43
Drive 129–30, 174
Druid 10
Dumfriesshire Foxhounds 14, *15*, 79, 156, 178
            Spendthrift 14, 17
Dunne Houndes 5

Ears 35, 41, 82, 85
Easebourne Tarquin, Dual Ch. *23*, 25
Edwards, Bobbie 34, *60*, 105, *127*, *142*, 146
Edwards, Henry *60*, *136*
Entropion 41, 42, 76, 176
Exercise 38, 48
Export 45
Expression 81, 84
Eyes 35, 82, 84–5
  bad 21, 76–8, 157, 217, 219

Farm stock 55, 59, 64–5, 129, 164
Faults 75–9, 176
Feeding 46–8
Feet 42, 83, 85, 157
Fitt, J. Nevill 9, 10, 12
Flags 123, 140
Foil 63
Foxhounds 8, 12, 14, 156, 158, 194
Fox hunting 8, 11, 13, 154
French Hound 17, 178
Furness, Eric 17, 79, 156, 157, 168, 173–78

Gait 82, 85, 86
Gaskins 83, 85, 86
Gascon-Saintongeois 178
German Shepherd dog 179, 205, 206, 219, 220
Gotwick Mettle, WT Ch. *28*, 31
Great Dane 12, 185
Greyhound 8
Griffon Vendeen 17
Growth, rate of *36*–7, 38, 47
Guarding 51

Handler 57, 59–62, 134–36, 147–53, 205
Hare foot 19

233

Harness 61, 69–71, 163
Health problems 35, 75–9, 176
Heath Hill Vermouth, WT
    Ch. *30*
Hebe, Ch. 13, 17
Hector II 197
Height 76, 83, 84
Hip displasia 75
Holmes, Sherlock 202
Horses for the judges 121
House training 49

Identification 72–3, 134, 163, 171
Importations 14–15, 177
Intermediate Stake 105, 106

Jack the Ripper 187–202, 203
Joynson, Lt Col. 17
Judges 110–12
    Assistant 112–13
Judge's Stewards 122–23
Judging 126–38, 160
Junior Stake 105, 106

Kelperland Trophy 107
Kennel Club of Great
    Britain 110, 111, 112, 120, 178, 180
    registration with 14, 16, 44–45
    Standard 81–83
    Working Trial Rules for
    Bloodhounds 105, 225–27
Kennel Club Tracking Certificate
    for Bloodhounds (Working
    Trial Certificate) 72, 105, 125, 134, 136, 146
Knightcall's Black Cherry 15
Krehl, George R. 200

Labrador 179, 205, 206, 219, 220
Land for trials 108–10
Landmarks 71, 125, 140

Lawyer 13, 17
Laying on 58, 68–69
Le Couteulx de Canteleu,
    Count 1, 4, 9, 177
Lead training 54–55
Leashes 69–71, 163
Licence 110
Life span 35
Lift 63, 65
Lip 78–79
Limiers 4, 8
Lines, planning 115–19
    walking 138–41
Lowe, Margaret 49, *135*
Luath XI 13, 17

Maddox, Bob *68*
Maps for trials 113–20
Markers 71
Matchley Berniston 186–87
    Venus 186–87
Maynard, Samuel 13, 184, 185
Metropolitan Police Dog
    Training Establishment 203
Morgan Jones, Lt Col.
    Keith 210–14
Moss-trooping 14, 17
Moulting 35
Mouth 79
Movement 74, 79, 91, 92, 96–100

Name 8
Napier, Ch. 13, 17
Nevill, Thomas 13, 17, 184
New Forest 13, 184, 204, 215
Nichols, E. 13, 17, 192
Nimrod 11
Novice Stake 105, 106, 165
North Warwickshire
    Bloodhounds 154, *155*, *161*

Obstacles 59, 63–64, 78, 132, 164, 220
Outcross 79, 156, 177–78

Packs, bloodhound 8–10, 169, 172
Pasterns *93, 95, 97, 98*
Peak Bloodhounds 14, 79, 168–171, 173–78
Pedigree 45
Penton Houdini, WT Ch. *33*
Pogodzinski, Leonarda 168–71
Points system 79–81
Police dogs 203–8
Prizegiving venue 121
Prizes 123, 137–38

Quarry 55, 56, 72, 138–41

Raycroft Jailer, WT Ch. *22*, 24, 177
    Jasmine, WT Ch. *24*, 177
    Rector 169
Ray's Victor 13, 17
Reading 61–63, 72, 167
Registration 14, 16, 44–45
Restless 13, 17
Restricted Working Permit 106
Riot 64, 128–29
Road crossing 116, 123
    Marshal 121–22
Royal Army Veterinary Corps 210, 216
Runner 60, 71, 123–25, 138–41, 146–47
Rushton Rochester, WT Ch. *32*, 169–70

Sagaces 80, 82
St Hubert (François Hubert) 2–4
St Hubert Hound 2, 4–7, 9, 17, 196
St Hubert's Day 4
Sanguine Abingerwood Tinsel, WT Ch. *26*, 29, *133*, *142*

Sanguine Sable 144
Saga *59, 60*
Saint, Ch. 36–37, 127
Saintly, WT Ch. *29, 40, 136*
Sally 77
Sanft *60*, 61
Sans Pareil *57*
Saturn, WT Ch. *31*, 146–53, *181*
Scent 65–67, 130, 141–46, 158–59, 167, 207–10
Schedules 112
Selman, S. *135*
Senior Stake 105, 106, 107, 111, 125, 146–53
Sewell, A. 193
Sherlock Sea Urchin, WT Ch. *27*
Shows 16, 21, 74–75, 79–81
Shylock of Stanwell *106*
Sickle hock *91*
Size 76, 83
Skin 82, 83, 86
    infections 35, 219
Slave hunting 12
Sleuth Hounds 7–8, 182
Smeller *57, 60*, 68
Solace 14, 17
Southern Hound 17
Speak (bay) 61, 74, 133, 167
Speed 131–32, 165
Stake Manager 122, 125–6
Stakes 105, 106, 165
Standard, The 1, 21, 41, 74–104
    Kennel Club of Great Britain 81–83
    American 83–86
Stern (tail) 41, 83, 85, 86, *88, 90*
Stifle 41, 75, 86–89, 157
Stringer, Major W. J. *11*
Strong, L. 17
Style 137
Summing up 121, 125, 126

Surveying 113–14
Sutcliffe, Nick *60*
Sutcliffe, Sue *61*

Talbot Hound 6–7, 8, 13, 17
Teeth and teething 50
Temperament 41, 43, 51, 81, 84, 213
Throw tongue 62, 133–34, 174
Tickell, Thomas 1
Toys 46, 50
Training, general 49–54, 162, 217, 218
   house 49
   hunt 55–73, 217
   lead 54–55
Trials 105–53
   early 16, *18–20*
Turner, Dr Sidney 21, 81

Vaccinations 38, 45, 50, 56
Voice 133–34, 174

Warren, Sir Charles 193, 195–201
Warwick Dog Show 16, 183, 197

Weight 75, 83, 84, 213
Westsummerland Montgomery of Bre-Mar-Har-Ros 14, 25, 27, 28, 29
Whyte-Melville 8, 175
Wildlife 59, 64–65, 138
Wilkinson, Chief Inspector 203
Windsor Forest Pack *11*
Winchell, J. L. 185–87
Wolverton, Lord 8, 9
Working Certificate 107
   Permit 106, 107, 165
   Trial Certificate (Tracking Certificate) 72, 105, 125, 134, 136, 146
   Trial Champions *22–33*, 105, 177
Wright, Reg R. 154–62, *160*, *175*
Wright, Mrs Reg *155*
Wrinkle 42, 76–78, 85, 176
Wuthering Cup *40*

Yeandle, Ex-Sergeant Major George 152, 214, *216*